English Grammar Made Easy

Step-by-step Lessons To Improve Your Writing and Speaking

Copyright 2016 by Poplin Publishing - All rights reserved.

This document is geared towards providing exact and reliable information in regards to the topic and issue covered. The publication is sold with the idea that the publisher is not required to render accounting, officially permitted, or otherwise, qualified services. If advice is necessary, legal or professional, a practiced individual in the profession should be ordered.

- From a Declaration of Principles which was accepted and approved equally by a Committee of the American Bar Association and a Committee of Publishers and Associations.

In no way is it legal to reproduce, duplicate, or transmit any part of this document in either electronic means or in printed format. Recording of this publication is strictly prohibited and any storage of this document is not allowed unless with written permission from the publisher. All rights reserved.

The information provided herein is stated to be truthful and consistent, in that any liability, in terms of inattention or otherwise, by any usage or abuse of any policies, processes, or directions contained within is the solitary and utter responsibility of the recipient reader. Under no circumstances will any legal responsibility or blame be held against the publisher for any reparation, damages, or monetary loss due to the information herein, either directly or indirectly.

Respective authors own all copyrights not held by the publisher.

The information herein is offered for informational purposes solely, and is universal as so. The presentation of the information is without contract or any type of guarantee assurance.

The trademarks that are used are without any consent, and the publication of the trademark is without permission or backing by the trademark owner. All trademarks and brands within this book are for clarifying purposes only and are the owned by the owners themselves, not affiliated with this document.

Credits – Images used in this publication are provided by the following;

(Photo by Jim and Becca Wicks, courtesy of Wikimedia Commons)

(Photo by pauliceko, courtesy of Pixabay)

(Photo by skeeze, courtesy of Pixabay)

(Photo by Samir Eberlin, courtesy of Wikimedia Commons)

(Photo by Chand Alli, courtesy of Wikimedia Commons)

(Photo by U.S. Navy Photographer's Mate 2nd Class Richard J. Brunson, courtesy of Wikimedia Commons)

ISBN: 9781521729632

Contents

Introduction 1

Contents 3

Chapter 1: How to use this book 1

Chapter 2: Nouns 5
   Lesson 1: Common nouns and proper nouns 5
   Lesson 2: Concrete nouns and abstract nouns 8
   Lesson 3: Countable and uncountable nouns 9
   Lesson 4: Singular and plural 11
   Lesson 5: Collective nouns 18
   Lesson 6: Gender nouns 26
   Lesson 7: Compound nouns 33
   Lesson 8: Noun cases 38

Chapter 3: Pronouns 44
   Lesson 9: Personal pronouns 44
   Lesson 10: Possessive pronouns 47
   Lesson 11: Demonstrative pronouns 49
   Lesson 12: Indefinite pronouns 50
   Lesson 13: Interrogative pronouns 51
   Lesson 14: Relative pronouns 54
   Lesson 15: Reflexive and intensive pronouns 57
   Lesson 16: Reciprocal pronouns 59

Chapter 4: Determiners 61
   Lesson 17: Articles 61
   Lesson 18: Demonstratives 63
   Lesson 19: Quantifiers 65
   Lesson 20: Possessives 68

Chapter 5: Verbs and verb tenses 70

Lesson 21: Action verbs and stative verbs 70
Lesson 22: Transitive verbs and intransitive verbs 73
Lesson 23: The present, past and past participle forms of verbs 75
Lesson 24: The infinitive 85
Lesson 25: Verb conjugation 87
Lesson 26: The –ing form of verbs 90
Lesson 27: Auxiliary verbs 94
Lesson 28: Modal verbs 96
Lesson 29: The simple verb tenses 102
Lesson 30: The progressive verb tenses 107
Lesson 31: The perfect verb tenses 110
Lesson 32: The perfect progressive verb tenses 115
Lesson 33: Contractions 119
Lesson 34: Phrasal verbs 124

Chapter 6: Adjectives 126

Lesson 35: Attributive, predicative and nominal adjectives 127
Lesson 36: Comparison 129
Lesson 37: The order of adjectives 134
Lesson 38: Adjective phrases 136

Chapter 7: Adverbs 137

Lesson 39: How to identify adverbs 137
Lesson 40: Kinds of adverbs 139
Lesson 41: Forming adverbs from adjectives 143
Lesson 42: Adverb phrases and adverb clauses 145

Chapter 8: Prepositions 147

Lesson 43: Types of prepositions 147
Lesson 44: Prepositional phrases 151
Lesson 45: Idiomatic expressions with prepositions 152

Chapter 9: Conjunctions 156
Lesson 46: Types of conjunctions.......... 156
Lesson 47: Conjunctive adverbs 161

Chapter 10: Interjections 164
Lesson 48: How to use interjections 164

Chapter 11: Check your knowledge 167

Answers to exercises 172

Conclusion 195

Introduction

Understanding the intricacies of English grammar can be a challenge, not only for people who speak English as an additional language but also for native speakers. However, getting it right when you write anything in the English language is important because it shows that you (know when to use the correct words at the correct time) pay attention to detail.

English Grammar Made Easy offers you a basic introduction to the grammar rules of English. It focuses on the different parts of speech and shows you how to use English correctly. The book is structured in the form of lessons, each ending with at least one short exercise to help you check your understanding of what you've learned in that lesson. At the end of the book you'll find longer exercises mixing everything together.

If you want to understand the basics of English grammar and improve your language skills, *English Grammar Made Easy* will guide you every step of the way.

Chapter 1: How to use this book

English Grammar Made Easy is a basic guide to English grammar, focusing on the different parts of speech. It explains various aspects of nouns, pronouns, determiners, verbs, adjectives, adverbs, prepositions, conjunctions and interjections to get you started in understanding the rules of grammar.

You can use this book in different ways:

- Begin at Lesson 1 and work your way through each lesson in the order that it appears; then do the exercises at the end of the book to check your understanding.

- If you feel you need to work on a specific part of speech, start with the relevant chapter. The lessons are arranged in order from the basics to the more complicated aspects of the part of speech that they cover.

- You can start with the comprehensive exercises at the back of the book to see which aspects you need to work on and then go to the relevant chapter or lesson.

- You may also use the book as a basic grammar reference guide.

There are many different resources that you can use in addition to this book. Most importantly is to invest in a good dictionary. Those published by Oxford University Press, Cambridge University Press and Longman are highly recommended if you're looking for a dictionary that covers the different varieties of English. For US English, the Merriam-Webster dictionaries are a good buy too. The

following article gives you some advice on how to choose a good dictionary for your needs:
http://www.antimoon.com/how/dictionary.htm

Two of the best grammar reference guides are:

- *The Elements of Style* by William Strunk Jr. and E.B. White: This guide focuses primarily on US English and is the go-to for American writers, editors and scholars.

- *Oxford Modern English Grammar* by Bas Aarts covers both British and US English.

You will also find hundreds of websites with grammar lessons, advice and exercises. The following are especially useful:

- Grammar-Monster (http://grammar-monster.com/)

- Education First (http://www.ef.com/english-resources/)

- British Council (https://learnenglish.britishcouncil.org/en/quick-grammar)

- Grammarly (https://www.grammarly.com/)

- GrammarBook (http://www.grammarbook.com/)

- Grammar Girl (http://www.quickanddirtytips.com/grammar-girl)

- The Chicago Manual of Style Online (http://www.chicagomanualofstyle.org/home.html)

A note on the different varieties of English

Like most languages, English has different regional dialects. However, because English is spoken in so many parts of the world, these regional differences can be quite big. This is partly because English-speaking settlers had to adopt new words for things that didn't exist in England, from kangaroos in Australia to raccoons in the United States. In addition, immigrants from other countries brought words from their own languages to the English spoken in the new colonies.

In written English, there are two main varieties of the language: UK English is used in the United Kingdom as well as in most countries that are also members of the British Commonwealth, while US English is used mainly in the USA. Apart from some words that are unique to each of these varieties, the main difference between the two is in the spelling of certain words. In UK English, for instance, we write "colour", "defence" and "theatre" while in US English we write "color", "defense" and "theater".

In the past, words like these could be spelled either way because they came to English from Latin and French, which spelled them in different ways. In the USA during the 1820s, however, Noah Webster compiled the dictionary that standardized US spelling and chose just one way of spelling each word. Rivalry between the Americans and the British meant that they continued to spell things differently over the years.

In terms of grammar, there may be slight differences among the varieties of English. We address these where relevant in this book. However, the basic rules of English grammar remain the same no matter where in the world you are and which variety of English you speak.

Chapter 2: Nouns

When we start talking, the first words we say are usually words like "Mama", "Dada", "cat", "ball", "doll", "banana", "shop" and "teddy". These words are nouns. They describe things, people, places, events and ideas or concepts. Nouns are the words we use to describe what we are talking about.

There are different types of nouns to describe different kinds of concepts. For example, we can group nouns into common nouns and proper nouns, concrete nouns and abstract nouns, countable nouns and uncountable nouns and collective nouns.

Lesson 1: Common nouns and proper nouns

The two main types of nouns are common nouns and proper nouns.

Common nouns

Common nouns are words we use for people, animals, things, places and ideas. However, we only use them in a generic sense. Examples of common nouns are: woman, man, mother, father, child, dog, cat, frog, singer, doctor, flower, river, mountain, church, temple, book, banana, newspaper, song, love, pride and happiness.

We do not usually write common nouns with an initial capital letter, unless they are at the start of a sentence or form part of a title.

Proper nouns

Proper nouns are names. They are the specific names we use for certain people, animals, objects, places, institutions or organizations, days and months, holidays and festivals, religions, languages and national or ethnic groups as well as books and other publications, movies, works of art and songs.

Your name, for instance, is a proper noun. So are these: John Smith, President Obama, Madonna, Kermit the Frog, Lassie, Microsoft, Porsche, the Rocky Mountains, the Atlantic Ocean, India, the United Nations, the European Union, the Catholic Church, Harvard University, Tuesday, Friday, July, November, Christmas, Ramadan, the Festival of Lights, Hinduism, Buddhism, English, French, the Germans, the Japanese, Cherokee, African Americans, *Wuthering Heights*, *The New York Times*, *Star Wars*, the painting "The Last Supper" and the song "Happy Birthday".

You may have noticed from the examples that we start proper nouns with a capital letter. This is to show that we are talking about something very specific. For example, when we write "the rocky mountains" we simply mean mountains that are rocky but when we write "the Rocky Mountains", we mean the famous mountain range in North America.

Look at how the meaning of a sentence can change when we identify the proper nouns:

> I love turkey. (Here the noun "turkey" means the meat of a kind of bird. It is a common noun.)

> I love Turkey. (Here the noun "Turkey" is the name of a country. It is a proper noun.)

Exercise 1

Say whether each of these nouns is a common noun or a proper noun:

door	lion	Madagascar	Cookie Monster	rain
Pizza Hut	Guitar Hero	guitar hero	basil	Basil

Exercise 2

Identify the nouns in these sentences and say whether they are common nouns or proper nouns:

1. My friend Jill loves basketball.

2. We went to Amritsar to see the Golden Temple.

3. Michael watches Game of Thrones on television every Sunday.

4. My aunt fasts on the Day of Atonement.

5. Love is the most important feeling.

Lesson 2: Concrete nouns and abstract nouns

Some nouns are concrete nouns while others are abstract nouns.

Concrete nouns

Concrete nouns are nouns for things that we can experience through one or more of our senses. When something is a concrete noun, we can see it, hear it, taste it, smell it or touch or feel it.

Examples of concrete nouns are: book, dog, tree, music, barking, the Liberty Bell, coffee, salt, cake, flames, sunshine.

Abstract nouns

Abstract nouns are nouns for things that we cannot experience through our senses. We cannot see, hear, taste, smell or touch them. They are nouns for feelings or emotions, ideas and concepts and beliefs.

Examples of abstract nouns are: happiness, love, hate, fear, freedom, culture, education, religion, faith.

Exercise 3

Identify the nouns in these sentences and say whether they are concrete nouns or abstract nouns:

1. The dog is happy.
2. I have a craving for chocolate.
3. Her childhood was filled with joy and love.
4. He always tries to speak the truth.
5. Their mother campaigns for justice, democracy, freedom and dignity.

Lesson 3: Countable and uncountable nouns

Some nouns are countable nouns while others are uncountable nouns.

Countable nouns

Countable nouns are nouns that describe something we can count. They can be singular, which means that there is only one of what they describe, or they can be plural, which means that there are two or more. Examples of nouns in their singular form are: kitten, tree, mountain, man, road, cherry, skirt. Examples of nouns in their plural form are: kittens, trees, mountains, men, roads, cherries, skirts.

Uncountable nouns

Uncountable nouns describe things we cannot count, for example: water, advice, furniture, garbage, sugar. We always use the singular form for these nouns.

We often use uncountable nouns together with countable nouns to show quantity. For example:

- Water: Experts say that you have to drink <u>eight glasses</u> of water every day.
- Advice: My grandmother gave me <u>a piece</u> of advice that was very useful.
- Furniture: The <u>one piece</u> of furniture in the room was a chair.
- Garbage: They had <u>four bags</u> of garbage after they cleaned the house.
- Sugar: Mom asked me to buy <u>two pounds</u> of sugar.

Exercise 4

Identify the nouns in these sentences and say whether they are countable nouns or uncountable nouns:

1. There is a fly on the ceiling.

2. The boy asked for a glass of milk.

3. My friend ate an entire box of cookies.

4. The sand on the beach is very hot.

5. I'm going to make a sandwich with some butter and a slice of cheese.

Lesson 4: Singular and plural

Countable nouns can be singular or plural. When the noun describes only one thing, person or place, it uses the singular form. When it describes two or more things, people or places, it uses the plural form.

There are different ways to form plurals.

With most nouns, we simply add an –s at the end to make the plural form. For example:

Singular	Plural
door	doors
candle	candles
cloud	clouds
book	books
egg	eggs

Some nouns are a little more complicated. Below, we discuss some basic guidelines for forming the plural of some of these special nouns. However, there are exceptions to every rule and often the only way to be sure what the correct plural form is, is to use a dictionary.

Nouns that end in –s, –ss, –ch, –sh, –x or –z

When a noun ends in a hissing sound like –s, –ss, –ch, –sh, –x or –z, we usually form the plural by adding –es. For example:

Singular	Plural
bus	buses
class	classes
church	churches
wish	wishes
tax	taxes
waltz	waltzes

However, for some words ending in –z we add another z too:

Singular	Plural
quiz	quizzes
fez	fezzes

Nouns that end in –f or –fe

When a noun ends in –f or –fe, we sometimes form the plural by taking away the f and adding –ves. For example:

Singular	Plural
calf	calves
leaf	leaves
thief	thieves
knife	knives
wife	wives

However, for some words ending in –f and for most words ending in –ff, we simply add an –s:

Singular	Plural
brief	brief**s**
chief	chief**s**
cliff	cliff**s**
whiff	whiff**s**

Nouns that end in –y

When a noun ends in –y, we need to look at the letter that comes immediately before the y to see how we should form the plural.

If the letter before the y is a consonant, we usually form the plural by taking away the y and adding –ies. For example:

Singular	Plural
baby	bab**ies**
democracy	democrac**ies**
lady	lad**ies**
reply	repl**ies**
mummy	mumm**ies**
granny	grann**ies**
poppy	popp**ies**
library	librar**ies**
posy	pos**ies**
liberty	libert**ies**
navy	nav**ies**
frenzy	frenz**ies**

If the letter immediately before the y is a vowel, we simply add an –s. For example:

Singular	Plural
way	way**s**
key	key**s**
toy	toy**s**
guy	guy**s**

Nouns that end in –o

When a noun ends in –o, we sometimes form the plural by adding –es. For example:

Singular	Plural
potato	potato**es**
tomato	tomato**es**
hero	hero**es**

However, sometimes we form the plural by simply adding –s. For example:

Singular	Plural
radio	radio**s**
video	video**s**
photo	photo**s**
piano	piano**s**

Nouns that remain the same in the plural form

Some nouns remain the same in the plural form. Examples are:

Singular	Plural
bison	bison
corps	corps
deer	deer
means	means
moose	moose
series	series
sheep	sheep
scissors	scissors
species	species

Nouns that change in other ways in the plural form

Some nouns change in other ways in the plural form. For example:

Singular	Plural
addendum	addenda
alga	algae
bacterium	bacteria
basis	bases
beau	beaux
cactus	cacti or cactuses

child	children
crisis	crises
criterion	criteria
die	dice
emphasis	emphases
foot	feet
goose	geese
louse	lice
man	men
mouse	mice
ox	oxen
person	people
phenomenon	phenomena
tableau	tableaux
tooth	teeth
woman	women

Exercise 5

Give the plural form of each of these nouns. You may use a dictionary to help you.

1. dog
2. chair
3. tray
4. umbrella
5. beehive
6. mongoose
7. half
8. fungus
9. fireman
10. nanny
11. jelly
12. oasis
13. appendix
14. memorandum
15. life
16. wolf
17. puppy
18. box
19. daisy
20. aircraft

Lesson 5: Collective nouns

A collective noun is a special noun that we use to describe a group of certain people or things. When there are many different people watching the same concert, for instance, we call them the audience. Other examples of collective nouns are: team, family, jury, group, council.

Often we use a very specific collective noun to describe a certain group. For example, we call a group of fish "a school of fish". Here is a list of some other collective nouns and the nouns we use them for:

Noun	Collective noun
actors	a **company** of actors; a **troupe** of actors
airplanes	a **fleet** of airplanes
alligators	a **congregation** of alligators
ants	a **colony** of ants; a **swarm** of ants
antelope	a **herd** of antelope
apes	a **troop** of apes; a **shrewdness** of apes
arrows	a **quiver** of arrows
asteroids	a **belt** of asteroids
baboons	a **troop** of baboons; a **flange** of baboons
bacteria	a **culture** of bacteria
badgers	a **colony** of badgers
bats	a **colony** of bats
bears	a **sloth** of bears; a **sleuth** of bears
beauties	a **bevy** of beauties

beavers	a **colony** of beavers; a **lodge** of beavers
bees	a **swarm** of bees; a **hive** of bees
bills	a **wad** of bills
birds	a **flock** of birds; a **flight** of birds
books	a **library** of books
butterflies	a **flutter** of butterflies; a **flight** of butterflies; a **rabble** of butterflies
camels	a **caravan** of camels; a **herd** of camels
candidates	a **slate** of candidates
cars	a **fleet** of cars
cards	a **deck** of cards
caterpillars	an **army** of caterpillars
cattle	a **herd** of cattle; a **drove** of cattle
cats	a **cluster** of cats; a **ponce** of cats; a **clowder** of cats
chicks	a **clutch** of chicks; a **peep** of chicks
circuits	a **bank** of circuits
cobras	a **quiver** of cobras
crocodiles	a **congregation** of crocodiles; a **bask** of crocodiles; a **float** of crocodiles
crows	a **murder** of crows
dogs	a **pack** of dogs
dolphins	a **school** of dolphins; a **pod** of dolphins
ducks (on land)	a **flock** of ducks; a **brace** of ducks

ducks (on water)	a **bunch** of ducks; a **paddling** of ducks; a **raft** of ducks
ducks (in flight)	a **skein** of ducks; a **string** of ducks; a **team** of ducks
eagles	a convocation of eagles
eggs	a **clutch** of eggs
elephants	a **herd** of elephants; a **memory** of elephants
experts	a **panel** of experts
fish	a **school** of fish
flamingoes	a **stand** of flamingoes
flowers	a **bouquet** of flowers
frogs	an **army** of frogs
geese (on land)	a **gaggle** of geese
geese (in flight)	a **skein** of geese; a **team** of geese; a **wedge** of geese
giraffes	a **corps** of giraffes; a **tower** of giraffes
gnats	a **cloud** of gnats
goats	a **trip** of goats; a **herd** of goats
grapes	a **bunch** of grapes
hamsters	a **horde** of hamsters
hawks (in large migrating groups)	a **kettle** of hawks; a **boil** of hawks; a **cauldron** of hawks
hedgehogs	an **array** of hedgehogs
hens	a **brood** of hens

hippopotamuses	a **herd** of hippopotamuses; a **bloat** of hippopotamuses; a **thunder** of hippopotamuses
horses	a **stable** of horses; a **stud** of horses
hyenas	a **clan** of hyenas
jellyfish	a **bloom** of jellyfish
kangaroos	a **mob** of kangaroos; a **troop** of kangaroos
kittens	a **litter** of kittens
lawyers	a **murder** of lawyers
lemurs	a **conspiracy** of lemurs
leopards	a **leap** of leopards
lions	a **pride** of lions
mice	a **nest** of mice; a **colony** of mice
monkeys	a **troop** of monkeys; a **tribe** of monkeys
mountains	a **range** of mountains
octopi	a **consortium** of octopi
owls	a parliament of owls
oxen	a **team** of oxen; a **yoke** of oxen
oysters	a **bed** of oysters
pigs	a **drove** of pigs; a **drift** of pigs
porcupines	a **prickle** of porcupines
puppies	a **litter** of puppies
sailors	a **crew** of sailors
sheep	a **flock** of sheep; a **herd** of sheep

ships	a **fleet** of ships; an **armada** of ships; a **flotilla** of ships
snakes	a **den** of snakes; a **bed** of snakes; a **pit** of snakes; a **nest** of snakes
soldiers	a **platoon** of soldiers; a **squad** of soldiers; a **company** of soldiers; an **army** of soldiers
sparrows	a **host** of sparrows; a **flight** of sparrows
stars	a **galaxy** of stars
students	a **class** of students
tests	a **battery** of tests
thieves	a **gang** of thieves
tigers	an **ambush** of tigers; a **streak** of tigers
toads	a **knot** of toads
trees	a **forest** of trees; a **grove** of trees; a **stand** of trees; a **thicket** of trees; an **orchard** of trees
trucks	a **convoy** of trucks
turkeys	a **rafter** of turkeys
turtles	a **bale** of turtles
vipers	a **nest** of vipers
whales	a **pod** of whales
witches	a **coven** of witches
wolves	a **pack** of wolves
worshippers	a **congregation** of worshippers
zebras	a **herd** of zebras

Exercise 6

Use a collective noun to say what is in each of these pictures.

For example: A school of fish

1.

2.

3.

4.

5.

Lesson 6: Gender nouns

Gender refers to whether a person or animal is female or male. Gender nouns are special nouns where the meaning tells us about the gender of the person or animal that the noun describes. For example, the noun "woman" tells us that we are talking about a human who is female, while the noun "rooster" tells us that we are talking about a chicken that is male.

Many nouns are gender neutral, which means that we use them for both females and males. Examples are: baby, cat, cousin, friend, teacher. We call these common gender nouns and we tend to use them when the gender of the person or animal we are talking about is unknown or is not really relevant. When a noun refers specifically to a female person or animal, we say that it is the feminine form of the noun. When a noun refers to a male person or animal, we say that it is the masculine form of the noun.

Here is a list of gender nouns. In many cases there are common gender nouns as well as feminine and masculine forms, but not always.

Common gender noun	Feminine form	Masculine form
person	woman	man
Family		
parent	mother	father
child	girl (in general) daughter (in relation to the parents)	boy (in general) son (in relation to the parents)

sibling	sister	brother
	aunt	uncle
	niece	nephew
spouse	wife	husband
	bride	bridegroom; groom
single person	spinster	bachelor

Occupations

actor	actress	actor
flight attendant	flight stewardess	flight steward
server	waitress	waiter
	witch	wizard
	priestess	priest
	nun	monk

Titles

	empress	emperor
monarch	queen	king
	princess	prince
	lady	lord
	duchess	duke
	countess	count
	czarina	czar
	mistress	master
	madam	Sir

Other nouns for people		
hero	heroine	hero
host	hostess	host
deity	goddess	god
heir	heiress	heir
Animals		
alligator	cow	bull
antelope	doe	buck
bear	sow; she-bear	boar
bird	hen	cock
buffalo	cow	bull
camel	cow	bull
caribou	doe	buck
cat	queen	tom
cattle	cow	bull
chicken	hen	rooster
chimpanzee	empress	blackback
coyote	bitch	dog
crab	hen; jenny	cock; jimmy
crocodile	cow	bull
deer	doe; hind; cow	buck; stag; bull
dog	bitch	dog
dolphin	cow	bull
donkey	jenny	jack

dragonfly	queen	king; drake
duck	duck	drake
dugong	cow	bull
elephant	cow	bull
elk	cow	bull
falcon	falcon	tiercel; tercel
ferret	jill	hob
fox	vixen	fox; tod; dog
gerbil	doe	buck
giraffe	cow	bull
goat	nanny; doe	billy; buck
goose	goose	gander
hamster	doe	buck
hare	doe; jill	buck; jack
hawk	hen	tiercel
hedgehog	sow	boar
hippopotamus	cow	bull
hornet	queen	drone
horse	mare	stallion
hyena	bitch	dog
jellyfish	sow	boar
kangaroo	doe; jill; flyer	buck; jack; boomer
leopard	leopardess	leopard
lion	lioness	lion

lobster	hen	cock
manatee	cow	bull
mole	sow	boar
moose	cow	bull
mouse	doe	buck
opossum	jill	jack
otter	sow	boar
peafowl	peahen	peacock
pig	sow	boar
porcupine	sow	boar
prairie dog	sow	boar
rabbit	doe	buck
raccoon	sow	boar
rat	doe; cow	buck; bull
red deer	hind	stag; hart
reindeer	cow	bull
rhinoceros	cow	bull
salmon	hen	cock
sea lion	cow	bull
seal	cow	bull
sheep	ewe	ram
skunk	sow	boar
sloth	sow	boar
squirrel	doe	buck

swan	pen	cob
termite	cow	bull
tiger	tigress	tiger
turkey	hen	gobbler; stag; tom
whale	cow	bull
wolf	she-wolf; bitch	dog
wolverine	angeline	wolverine
wombat	jill	jack
yak	cow	bull
zebra	mare	stallion

Many nouns cannot be masculine or feminine. Examples are: computer, table, cloud, cookie, pillow. These nouns usually describe things and we call them neuter nouns.

Exercise 7

Say whether each of these nouns is masculine, feminine, a common gender noun or neuter:

1. queen
2. dove
3. airplane
4. goat
5. boar
6. gander
7. mare
8. sheep
9. door
10. flight attendant

Exercise 8

Give the opposite gender noun for each of these gender nouns. For example:

    duke: duchess

1. countess
2. hero
3. wolverine
4. jack
5. rooster
6. czar
7. stallion
8. nanny
9. ram
10. nun

Lesson 7: Compound nouns

We can combine two or more words to form a new noun. Nouns that consist of two or more different words are compound nouns.

A compound noun usually has two parts. The most important part is the one that describes the what or who. We call this part the head. The other part gives us a little more detail about the what or who. It tells us what kind the what or who is, or what its purpose is. We call this part the modifier.

Let us look at the word "bus driver" as an example. The head of this compound noun is "driver" and it tells us that the noun describes someone who drives something. The modifier, "bus", tells us that the driver is driving a bus.

Another example of a compound noun is "corkscrew". The head, "screw", tells us that the object is a kind of screw. The modifier, "cork", tells us what the screw does or what its purpose is: it pulls out corks.

In most compound nouns, the head is the second part of the compound noun and the modifier is the first part. However, sometimes the head is first and the modifier is second. Examples are: sergeant major, passer-by.

Types of compound nouns

There are three different kinds of compound nouns: the closed or solid compound noun, the hyphenated compound noun and the open or spaced compound noun.

- The closed or solid compound noun is a compound noun that we write as one word. For example: football, sunrise, wallpaper.

- The hyphenated compound noun is a compound noun that we write with hyphens between the different parts. For example: six-pack, mother-in-law.

- The open or spaced compound noun is a compound noun that we write as separate words. For example: flight attendant, swimming pool.

We can also form compound nouns that are a combination of these types. An example is: part-time singer.

There are no specific rules to tell us if we should write a compound noun as one word, with a hyphen or as separate words. The only way to know is by using a dictionary and even then we might have a choice of how we would prefer to write the compound noun.

A good rule of thumb is to write the compound noun as one word or with a hyphen if there is any chance of confusion. For example, the phrase "red head" is not necessarily a compound noun. It could simply describe a head that is red. If we want a compound noun for a person with red hair, we can write it as one word, "redhead", to make it clear that it is a compound noun.

How to form compound nouns

There are different ways to form compound nouns. For example:

- Noun–noun compound nouns consist of two different nouns. Examples are: toothpaste, bookshelf, teaspoon, railway, water tank, beauty queen.

- Verb–noun compound nouns consist of a verb as the modifier and a noun as the head. Examples are: breakfast, spoilsport, pickpocket, washing machine, know-nothing.

- Noun–verb compound nouns consist of a noun as the modifier and a verb as the head. Examples are: haircut, rainfall, sunshine.

- Adjective–noun compound nouns consist of an adjective as the modifier and a noun as the head. For example: bluebottle, greenhouse, software, latecomer, dry-cleaning.

- Noun–adjective compound nouns consist of a noun as the modifier and an adjective as the head. For example: teaspoonful.

- Preposition–noun compound nouns consist of a preposition as the modifier and a noun as the head. For example: bystander, upper class, overcoat, inside, afternoon.

How to tell if it really is a compound noun

It is easy to identify a compound noun when it is a proper noun too, because we use capital letters. The "White House", for instance, is clearly a compound noun because it is the name we use for the house where the President of the United States lives. A "white house" is simply a noun, "house", with an adjective, "white": it is a house that is white.

When the compound noun is a common noun, however, it can be more difficult to tell it apart from a noun with an adjective or preposition. However, when we pronounce a compound noun, we usually stress the first part or the modifier. For example, when we say "*green*house" with the stress on "green", we mean a building where plants grow inside. This is a compound noun. If, however, we say "green *house*" with the stress on "house", we mean a house that is green. This is not a compound noun but instead a noun with an adjective.

How to form plurals of compound nouns

To make a plural of a compound noun, we first need to identify the head. Then we turn only that part of the compound noun into a plural.

For example, the head of the compound noun "toothbrush" is "brush". To make the plural of "toothbrush", we only turn the head, which is "brush", into a plural. We keep the modifier, which is "tooth", in the singular form. So, the plural of "toothbrush" is not "teethbrushes" but it is "toothbrushes".

With most compound nouns, the head is the last part of the compound noun, so making the plural form is quite straightforward. Examples of compound-noun plurals are: tea**cups**, compound **nouns**, police**men**, sea**horses**, has-**beens**, teaspoon**fuls**.

When the head of the compound noun is not the last part of that noun, the plural form will depend on where in the compound noun we find the head, for example: **sergeants** major, assistant **secretaries** of state.

Exercise 9

Identify the compound nouns in these sentences:

1. We went window shopping at the new mall.
2. My friend got seven cards on Valentine's Day.
3. Next year my little brother and I will go on a road trip to the Blue Mountains.
4. The blackbird is a black bird.
5. Sam loves winter sports like snow-boarding and cross-country skiing.

Exercise 10

Make compound nouns to fit the definitions. For example:

    a box for carrying your lunch in: lunchbox

1. a room for storing things in
2. the size of the dress
3. a frame for fitting a window in
4. food for pets
5. a surgeon who operates on people's hearts

Exercise 11

Give the plural of each of these compound nouns:

1. bridegroom
2. birthday present
3. bucketful
4. assistant football coach
6. lady-in-waiting

Lesson 8: Noun cases

A simple sentence usually has three parts: the subject, the verb and the object. For example:

> John eats a cookie.

- The subject is the part of the sentence that is doing the action. In the example, the subject is "John", because John is the one doing the action.

- The verb is the part that describes the action. In the example, the verb is "eats" because the action is what John is doing, which is eating.

- The object is the part of the sentence that experiences the action. It I the part that the action is being done upon. In the example, the object is "a cookie". The cookie is not doing any action but it is experiencing the action: it is being eaten.

When we talk about noun cases, we mean the different forms that the noun takes depending on where it is in a sentence. In English, there are three cases: the nominative or subjective case, the accusative or objective case and the genitive or possessive case.

Nominative or subjective case

The nominative or subjective case is the form that the noun takes when it is the subject of the sentence. For example:

> The girl works on the computer.

In this sentence, the subject is "the girl" and the noun "girl" is in the nominative case.

We also use the nominative case of the noun in other ways:

- When the noun is a form of address:

    Mandy, come and eat your breakfast. ("Mandy" is a noun in the nominative case.)

    Man, it is hot! ("Man" is a noun in the nominative case.)

- When the noun is a predicate, which means that it follows a linking verb – usually the verb "to be" in its correct verb form – and renames the subject:

    Annie is a writer. (The noun "writer" is a predicate noun because it follows the linking verb "is" and renames "Annie", the subject.)

    Mike and Jeff are brothers. (The noun "brothers" is a predicate noun because it follows the linking verb "are" and renames "Mike and Jeff".)

- When the noun is an appositive, which means that it is a noun or noun phrase directly beside the subject and renames the subject:

    Annie, a writer, loves books. (The appositive is "a writer" because it renames "Annie", the subject, and "writer" is a noun in the nominative case.)

    Mike and Jeff, two brothers, live in Alaska. (The appositive is "two brothers" because it renames "Mike and Jeff", the subject, and "brothers" is a noun in the nominative case.)

Accusative or objective case

The accusative or objective case is the form that the noun takes when it is part of the object of the sentence. We can use the accusative or objective case in three ways:

- When it is a direct object, which means that it answers the question *What?* or *Whom?*:

    John eats a cookie. (What does John eat? A cookie. The direct object is "a cookie" because it answers the question *What?* The noun "cookie" takes the accusative or objective case.

- When it is an indirect object, which means that it answers the question *To what?*, *To whom?*, *For what?* or *For whom?*:

    I gave John a cookie. (To whom did I give a cookie? John. "John" is the indirect object because it answers the question *To whom?* and it takes the accusative or objective case. The direct object in this sentence is "a cookie" because it answers the question *What?*)

- When it is an object of a preposition:

    John eats in the dining room. (The preposition is "in" and the object of the preposition is "the dining room", so the noun "dining room" takes the accusative or objective case.)

Genitive or possessive case

The genitive or possessive case is the form that the noun takes when it shows ownership. Another term we can use for nouns in the genitive or possessive case is possessive nouns.

In reality, nouns usually look the same whether they are in the nominative or in the accusative case. However, they change form when they are possessive nouns. Here are the rules for forming possessive nouns:

- For a singular noun that does not end in an s or z, we add an apostrophe and an s: **'s**. For example: the **dog's** bone, **Mary's** lamb, the **world's** end.

- For a plural noun that does not end in an s, we add an apostrophe and an s: **'s**. For example: the **children's** toys, the **women's** cars.

- For a singular noun that ends in an s or a z, we can add an apostrophe with an s or we can just add an apostrophe. For example: **Chris's** shoes or **Chris'** shoes, the **class's** results or the **class'** results, **Mr Sanchez's** house or **Mr Sanchez'** house. The most important is that we are consistent in whichever way we choose to write the possessive noun.

- For a plural noun that ends in an s, we add an apostrophe: **'**. For example: The **dogs'** bones, the **buses'** wheels, the **Joneses'** cat, the **Sanchezes'** house.

- For nouns that are made up of acronyms or abbreviations, we follow the same rules as for regular singular nouns. For example: **NASA's** astronauts, the **FBI's** agents, the **TV's** antenna, **AIDS's** effects or **AIDS'** effects.

- For compound nouns, we add the apostrophe at the end of the compound noun, no matter whether that is the head or the modifier. We then follow the same rules about adding an s to the apostrophe as we do for regular singular or plural nouns. For example: the **sunrise's** colors, the **sergeant major's** uniform, the **sergeants major's** uniforms, the **sausage dogs'** bones, the **cutlass's blade** or the **cutlass' blade**.

- When two or more nouns share the same possession, we show possession only after the last noun. For example: the **dog** and **cat's** owner; **Tom**, **Dick** and **Harry's** mother.

- When two or more nouns do not share the same possession, we indicate possession separately for each noun. For example: the **dog's** and **cat's** bowls, **Tom's**, **Dick's** and **Harry's** wives.

A common mistake in English is to use an apostrophe to indicate a plural form. We call this the greengrocer's apostrophe because greengrocers often use it on their signs: apple's, pear's, banana's. However, we never use an apostrophe to indicate plural, except in three cases:

- The plural of single letters. For example: crossing the t's and dotting the i's.

- The plural of numbers written as digits. For example: all the number 7's.

- The plural of symbols. For example: all the *'s and #'s in this text.

Exercise 12

Identify the nouns in the nominative case in each of these sentences:

1. Mandy likes Joe.

2. Mandy, Joe is here!

3. Mandy, a friend, likes Joe.

4. Mandy is my friend.

5. Joe is a handsome man.

Exercise 13

Identify the nouns in the accusative case in each of these sentences:

1. Stuart is watching *Game of Thrones*.
2. Stuart is eating popcorn too.
3. Stuart is my brother and he loves popcorn.
4. I made Stuart some popcorn to eat while he watches *Game of Thrones* on television.
5. I prefer pizza.

Exercise 14

Identify the possessive nouns in each of these sentences:

1. Rachel and I are eating at Tom's new restaurant.
2. Rachel's favorite food is pasta with pesto.
3. The menus are in English and Italian because many of the restaurant's customers are from Italy.
4. The servers' uniforms were designed by Tom's wife.
5. There's a fly in my soup but not in Rachel's.

Exercise 15

Give the possessive form of the nouns in brackets:

1. (Barbara) dog and cat are best friends.
2. The (dog) name is Spot and the (cat) name is Socks.
3. The (dog and cat) favorite thing is to play with each other.
4. The (dog and cat) food bowls are next to each other.
5. The (neighbors) children love watching the (Spot and Socks) unusual friendship.

Chapter 3: Pronouns

Pronouns are special words that we can use in place of nouns. Without pronouns, we would have to keep repeating the nouns over and over again. For example, look at this sentence:

> Karl wants Karl's daughter to replace Karl as director of Karl's company.

This sentence is very clumsy. By using pronouns, however, we can make the sentence much easier to read and understand:

> Karl wants his daughter to replace him as director of his company.

Pronouns usually have a clear antecedent, which is the noun that they replace. In the sentence above, the pronouns are "his" and "him" while the antecedent, the noun that they replace, is "Karl".

There are different kinds of pronouns, including personal pronouns, possessive pronouns, demonstrative pronouns, indefinite pronouns, interrogative pronouns, relative pronouns, reflexive pronouns, intensive pronouns and reciprocal pronouns.

Lesson 9: Personal pronouns

Personal pronouns are pronouns we use for grammatical person, which can be first person, second person or third person:

- First person refers to the speaker or speakers: I or we.
- Second person refers to the person or people being addressed: you.

- Third person refers to a person or people other than the speaker or the person being addressed: he, she, it or they.

Personal pronouns tell us more about the person or people we are talking about, how many of them there are and what their gender is.

Personal pronoun cases

Like nouns, personal pronouns can act as subject or object in a sentence. They can take the nominative or subject case or they can take the oblique or object case. However, while nouns do not change form whether they are subject or object, personal pronouns do.

		Singular		**Plural**	
		Subject pronoun	**Object pronoun**	**Subject pronoun**	**Object pronoun**
First person		I	me	we	us
Second person		you	you	you	you
Third person				they	them
	Male	he	him		
	Female	she	her		
	Neuter	it	it		

Here are some examples of personal pronouns in sentences, with the subject pronouns underlined and the object pronouns in italics:

<u>I</u> like *you*.

<u>You</u> like *me*.

<u>He</u> likes *her*.

<u>She</u> likes *him*.

<u>It</u> likes *us*.

<u>We</u> like *it*.

<u>You</u> like *them*.

<u>They</u> like *you*.

Exercise 16

Replace the words in brackets with the correct personal pronoun. For example:

Mary likes David very much. In fact, (Mary) loves (David).

Mary likes David very much. In fact, <u>she</u> loves *him*.

1. Ms Naidoo has a green marker pen. (Ms Naidoo) uses (the green marker pen) to write on the whiteboard.
2. My friend and I love watching movies. (My friend and I) like comedies best. (Comedies) are funny.
3. Andrew, would (Andrew) like a cookie? (The cookie) is still warm from the oven.
4. The dogs next door are not very friendly. (The dogs) are always barking at (Gina and I). (Gina and I) are scared of (the dogs).
5. Kathy and Diana, come and look at the rainbow. Can (Kathy and Diana) see (the rainbow)?

Lesson 10: Possessive pronouns

Possessive pronouns are similar to possessive nouns in that they indicate possession. However, unlike possessive nouns, possessive pronouns do not contain apostrophes.

Possessive pronouns can stand alone. They do not have to go with a noun. We use these pronouns to avoid repetition. For example, look at this sentence:

> The house is not his house; it is her house.

By using possessive pronouns, we can avoid using the word "house" three times in one sentence:

> The house is not <u>his</u>; it is <u>hers</u>.

These are the possessive pronouns:

		Singular	**Plural**
		Possessive pronoun	**Possessive pronoun**
First person		mine	ours
Second person		yours	yours
Third person			theirs
	Male	his	
	Female	hers	
	Neuter	its	

Here are examples of how we can use possessive pronouns in sentences:

> This book is <u>mine</u>.
>
> This book is <u>yours</u>.
>
> This book is <u>his</u>.
>
> This book is <u>hers</u>.
>
> This book is <u>its</u>.
>
> This book is <u>ours</u>.
>
> This book is <u>yours</u>.
>
> This book is <u>theirs</u>.

Remember that a possessive pronoun never has an apostrophe.

Exercise 17

Replace the personal pronouns in brackets with the appropriate possessive pronouns. For example:

> The guitar is (I).
>
> The guitar is <u>mine</u>.

1. Those are Paul's shoes. The shirt is (he) too.
2. Tina is wearing a dress that is (you).
3. Those bags are (we)!
4. The girls think that the cake is (they).
5. Maureen is looking for her phone. Do you know if this one is (she)?

Lesson 11: Demonstrative pronouns

We use demonstrative pronouns to point out specific things. There are only four demonstrative pronouns: this, these, that, those.

- To point out things that are near in space or time, we use "this" for one thing and "these" for two or more things. For example:

  This is my book right here. These are my crayons next to my book.

- To point out things that are farther away in space or time, we use "that" for one thing and "those" for two or more things.

  That is my book on the table over there. Those are my crayons next to my book.

Because we use demonstrative pronouns in the place of nouns, they stand alone. They do not go together with nouns. When the words "this", "these", "that" or "those" appear directly before a noun, for example "this hat" or "those shoes", they are determiners, which we will discuss in Chapter 4.

Exercise 18

Underline the demonstrative pronouns in these sentences:

1. I cannot believe this!
2. Are these your keys?
3. That was so much fun!
4. Those are the shoes that I want.
5. These apples look a little rotten. Those look much fresher.

Lesson 12: Indefinite pronouns

Indefinite pronouns are the opposite of demonstrative pronouns in that they do not refer to any specific thing or person. Examples of indefinite pronouns are: each, every, everyone, everybody, everything, any, anyone, anybody, anything, some, someone, somebody, something, no, none, no one, nobody, nothing, many, few, several, all, much, most, both, one, others, either, neither.

Like demonstrative pronouns, indefinite pronouns stand on their own, taking the place of a noun. If they appear right before a noun, they are not indefinite pronouns; instead, they are adjectives, which we will discuss in Chapter 6.

Exercise 19

Underline the indefinite pronouns in these sentences:

1. Somebody is playing loud music.

2. How would one bake a cake without an oven?

3. Come on, everybody, let's do something about this!

4. I don't want to eat anything. Neither does she.

5. Both boys are twelve years old. Both love riding their bicycles.

Lesson 13: Interrogative pronouns

Interrogative pronouns are pronouns that we use to ask questions. They represent the nouns that we ask the questions about. Sometimes the questions can be direct and have a question mark at the end but other times they are indirect questions within a sentence.

In English, there are five interrogative pronouns. The interrogative pronouns are: what, which, who, whom, whose.

- What: We use the interrogative pronoun "what" to ask about people or things. For example:

  What would you like to eat?

  What is your name?

  I wonder what time it is.

- Which: We use the interrogative pronoun "which" to ask about people or things too, but "which" usually indicates that there are different options to choose from. For example:

  Which cookie would you like?

  Which of these girls is your sister?

  The man asked which bus to take to the city.

- Who: We use the interrogative pronoun "who" to ask about the identity of people. For example:

  Who is that boy over there?

  Who took my umbrella?

  I wonder who is knocking on the door.

- Whom: We use the interrogative pronoun to ask about the identity of people too, but "whom" indicates that the person is the object of the sentence. For example:

    Whom did you call last night?

    Whom are you going with?

    I cannot decide whom to vote for.

- Whose: We use the interrogative pronoun "whose" to ask about the identity of people as well, but "whose" is always about possession. For example:

    Whose keys are these?

    Whose cat is that?

    I wonder whose baby is crying like that.

We can also use variations of the five interrogative pronouns by adding *–ever* or *–soever* at the end. For example:

- Whatever is that?
- Whichever cookie will I choose?
- Whosoever is calling this late?
- Whomsoever did you speak to at the party?
- Whosever keys could these be?

It is important to remember that when the pronoun does not ask a question and when it does not relate to a noun, it is not an interrogative pronoun. Question words like "why", "how" and "where", for instance, are not interrogative pronouns because they do not represent or replace nouns. Instead, they are interrogative adverbs, which we discuss in Lesson 40.

Exercise 20

Identify and underline the interrogative pronouns in the following paragraphs:

I was really excited about going to the party. <u>Who</u> would be there? <u>Whom</u> would I meet?

The entire afternoon I spent wondering what to wear. <u>Which</u> dress would be more flattering: the green one or the red one? <u>Which</u> shoes would be the most comfortable for dancing in but would still look great? How would I do my hair? Would I wear it in a ponytail, a bun or just let it flow loosely over my shoulders?

When I finally got dressed and was ready to go, disaster struck! Where were my keys? They were not where I always left them on the table by the front door. <u>Whosoever</u> could have taken them? I searched and searched, knowing that if I didn't find my keys soon, I would not be able to go at all. <u>What</u> would my friends think? How would the birthday girl feel if I didn't show up?

After what felt like hours, I heard something tinkling in the living room. <u>Whatever</u> could that be? I went to take a look and there, playing with my bunch of keys, was the biggest ginger cat I had ever seen. Now I had something new to worry about: <u>Whose</u> cat was it?

Lesson 14: Relative pronouns

Relative pronouns are pronouns that we use to join sentences. They introduce adjective clauses.

What is an adjective clause?

An adjective clause, also known as a relative clause, is a phrase that describes a noun. It can identify the noun or it can give us more information about the noun.

- An adjective clause that identifies a noun follows the noun and tells us who or what we are talking about. For example:

  The girl who sells lemonade is walking down the street. (The noun is "girl".)

  The horse which always tries to bite my arm is in the stable. (The noun is "horse".)

  The cup that has a crack in it is on the table. (The noun is "cup".)

- An adjective clause that gives us more information about a noun follows the noun too. It doesn't help us identify the noun but tells us more about the noun. For example:

  The boy, who is eleven years old, likes skateboarding. (The noun is "boy".)

  The boy puts his jeans, which are now dirty and torn, in the washing machine. (The noun is "jeans".)

The relative pronouns

In the example sentences above, you will see that each adjective clause starts with a word like "who", "which" or "that". These words are the relative pronouns because they introduce the adjective clauses and link them to the nouns they describe.

We use certain relative pronouns to refer to people, certain relative pronouns to refer to things and certain relative pronouns to refer to people or things. Like nouns and personal pronouns, relative pronouns can change according to grammatical case. These are the relative pronouns:

What does the pronoun refer to?	Nominative or subjective case	Accusative or objective case	Genitive or possessive case
People	who For example: The girl <u>who</u> sells lemonade	whom For example: The boy <u>whom</u> she sells lemonade to	whose For example: The girl <u>whose</u> lemonade is delicious
Things	which For example: The jeans <u>that</u> tore	which For example: The jeans <u>that</u> the boy tore	whose For example: The jeans <u>whose</u> fabric is torn
People or things	that For example: The boy <u>that</u> likes skateboarding The horse <u>that</u> tries to bite me	that For example: The boy <u>that</u> I saw falling The horse <u>that</u> I hate	whose For example: The boy <u>whose</u> jeans tore The horse <u>whose</u> teeth are sharp

Like with the interrogative pronouns, we can also add –*ever* or –*soever* to the relative pronouns who, whom, which and whose.

Exercise 21

Identify the relative pronouns in these sentences:

1. Mr Winter, who loves cooking, owns a restaurant.

2. The chicken that Mr Winter cooked is on the table.

3. The dog, whose owner is not here, is going into the kitchen.

4. The dog which has stolen the chicken is now eating it.

5. Whoever is that woman whom Mr Winter is talking to?

Exercise 22

Fill in the relative pronouns in these sentences:

1. I went to the party _____ Kevin threw.

2. I wore my new dress _____ is white.

3. Kevin, _____ birthday it was, had a chocolate birthday cake.

4. I spilled some cake _____ was creamy and delicious on my dress.

5. My dress, _____ price was actually more than I could afford, is now stained.

Lesson 15: Reflexive and intensive pronouns

Reflexive and intensive pronouns are the "self" pronouns. They end with *–self* or *–selves*. They cannot stand alone but always have to appear with a pronoun already in the sentence.

Reflexive pronouns

A reflexive pronoun reflects back to a pronoun or noun that acts as the subject of a sentence. The reflexive pronoun forms the object of the sentence but it has to refer to the same person or thing as the subject of the sentence. For example:

> I wash myself. I do not wash anybody else.
>
> You wash yourself.
>
> The boy washes himself.
>
> The girl washes herself.
>
> The cat washes itself.
>
> We wash ourselves.
>
> You wash yourselves.
>
> They wash themselves.

Intensive pronouns

Like the reflexive pronouns, the intensive pronouns are: myself, yourself, himself, herself, itself, ourselves, yourselves and themselves.

However, intensive pronouns intensify or emphasize the antecedents they refer to. For example:

> I myself made the coffee. Nobody else made the coffee; I did it.

Telling reflexive and intensive pronouns apart

Because they look so similar, it can be easy to confuse reflexive and intensive pronouns. To know the difference, we can ask ourselves these questions:

- Who does the subject of the sentence do the action to? If it is to the subject and to nobody else, we are dealing with a reflexive pronoun:

    I did it *to* <u>myself</u> and not to anybody else.

- Who is doing the action? If it is the subject of the sentence and nobody else, we are dealing with an intensive pronoun:

    I did it <u>myself</u>; nobody else did.

Exercise 23

Fill in the right reflexive or intensive pronoun in these sentences:

1. Jim drives _____ to work every day.

2. I made your birthday card _____.

3. It is funny to watch kittens learning how to wash _____.

4. We _____ wrote that song.

5. Candice, that was good work! Give _____ a pat on the shoulder.

Exercise 24

Say whether the underlined pronouns in these sentences are reflexive or intensive pronouns:

1. The kids <u>themselves</u> could not believe what was happening.
2. Sometimes you have to ask <u>yourself</u> if you really know what you are doing.
3. I wish more people would think for <u>themselves</u>.
4. Do you think we could build a house like that <u>ourselves</u>?
5. Sandy made <u>herself</u> a sandwich and then she ate it <u>herself</u>.

Lesson 16: Reciprocal pronouns

We use reciprocal pronouns to indicate that two or more people are carrying out some kind of action and that the action affects them all in the same way. They can receive the same benefits, for example, or suffer the same consequences. The action is mutual.

The reciprocal pronouns in English are: each other, one another.

- We use "each other" when there are only two parties involved in the action. For example:

    Nick and Mike do not like <u>each other</u>. (Nick does not like Mike and Mike does not like Nick.)

    Karl and Trish gave <u>each other</u> presents on their anniversary. (Karl gave Trish a present and Trish gave Karl a present.)

    The Russians and the Germans fought <u>each other</u> during the war. (The Russians fought the Germans and the Germans fought the Russians.)

- We use "one another" when there are more than two parties involved in the action or when we do not know how many people are involved. For example:

   Kathy, Diana and Shirley love spending time with <u>one another</u>. (Kathy loves spending time with Diana and Shirley; Diana loves spending time with Kathy and Shirley; Shirley loves spending time with Kathy and Diana.)

   The players from the different teams congratulated <u>one another</u> after the match.

   All the children help <u>one another</u> with the exercises.

Reciprocal pronouns can have possessive forms too. For example:

   Angie and Lea sometimes wear <u>each other's</u> clothes. Angie sometimes wears Lea's clothes and Lea sometimes wears Angie's clothes.

   All of Anita's cats play with <u>one another's</u> toys.

Exercise 25

Fill in the correct reciprocal pronouns in these sentences:

1. It was raining when we said goodbye to _____ outside the school gates.
2. Kyle and I accidentally took _____ umbrellas.
3. We heard a loud crash and Kyle and I looked first at _____, then toward where two cars had just crashed into _____.
4. The drivers of the two cars were shouting at _____.
5. Kyle and I spoke to the drivers and then we all took _____ contact details.

Chapter 4: Determiners

Determiners are special words that we use to introduce nouns and place them into context. They always go with nouns.

There are many different determiners in English. We can group them into articles, demonstratives, quantifiers and possessives.

Lesson 17: Articles

Articles are the words we use most often in English. There are two kinds of articles: the definite article and the indefinite articles.

The definite article

There is only one definite article in English: the. This little word tells us that the noun or noun phrase that we are talking about is a specific one. For example:

> The owl is hooting.

We are not talking about just any owl but about a specific owl.

The indefinite articles

The indefinite articles are "a" and "an". When they appear before a noun or noun phrase, we know that we are not talking about the noun in a specific sense but in a more general sense. For example:

> A bird is singing.

We do not know which specific bird is singing.

- We use "a" when the noun or noun phrase that follows it starts with a consonant sound. For example:

  There is <u>a</u> *fly* in my soup.

  There is <u>a</u> **big**, *black fly* in my soup.

- We use "an" when the noun or noun phrase that follows it starts with a vowel sound. For example:

  There is <u>an</u> ***ant*** on my sandwich.

  There is <u>an</u> ***ugly*** *ant* on my sandwich.

Sometimes we have to say the noun or noun phrase out loud because even though it might start with a consonant when it is written, the way we pronounce it may be a vowel sound. For example:

I will see you in half <u>an</u> hour.

Danny would like to become <u>an</u> FBI agent when he grows up.

Note that in American English, we often pronounce words differently than in British English. The word "herb", for example, is pronounced as "erb" in the USA and as "herb" in the UK. So, in American English we will say "an herb" and in British English we will say "a herb".

Exercise 26

Fill in the correct definite or indefinite article in the following sentences:

1. There is _____ bird in _____ tree outside my window. _____ bird is singing _____ beautiful song.

2. I would love to have _____ elephant as _____ pet.

3. It was on _____ weather report on TV tonight that there is _____ hurricane on the way.

4. When he realized that his ship was going to sink, _____ captain sent _____ SOS to call for help.

5. There is _____ hermit who lives about _____ hour's walk into _____ woods near my house.

Lesson 18: Demonstratives

In Chapter 3 we discussed the demonstrative pronouns "this", "these", "that" and "those". We can also use these words as determiners.

When we use the demonstratives as determiners, they do not stand alone. Instead, they always go with a noun. The noun normally follows directly after the demonstrative determiner. For example:

This dog is mine.

The noun "dog" follows directly after the determiner "This". Compare this to the following sentence, where we use "this" as a demonstrative noun which can stand alone:

This is my dog.

Exercise 27

Underline the demonstratives in the following paragraphs:

<u>These</u> days, I prefer to spend Friday night at home with a good book or a movie. Sometimes I will treat myself and order one of <u>those</u> pizzas with every topping I can think of and some extra cheese. <u>This</u> is my idea of a party now that I'm older.

Back when I was a student in my twenties, <u>this</u> kind of Friday night was my biggest nightmare. Weekends were party time! I will always remember <u>that</u> time when we went to a music festival and danced to <u>this</u> band that played the craziest music with fiddles and didgeridoos. It was freezing <u>that</u> night but we stayed warm simply by dancing until sunrise. <u>Those</u> were the days!

Lesson 19: Quantifiers

Quantifiers are determiners that we use to tell us how many of the noun we are talking about. There are many different quantifiers. For example:

<u>Each</u> child got a cupcake.

I would like <u>a little</u> milk with my tea, please.

Would you like <u>some</u> orange juice?

Some quantifiers can only go with countable nouns; some can only go with uncountable nouns and others can go with any kind of noun.

- Quantifiers that can go only with countable nouns: each, either, neither, both, few, a few, several, a couple of, hundreds of, thousands of, millions of

- Quantifiers that can only go with uncountable nouns: a little, a bit of, much, not much, a great deal of, a good deal of

- Quantifiers that can go with countable or uncountable nouns: all, any, no, none of, enough, more, most, less, a lot of, lots of, some, plenty of, heaps of, tons of, loads of, a load of

Quantifiers for groups

When we are talking about members of groups in general, we place the noun directly after the quantifier. For example:

<u>Few</u> cats like to swim.

<u>All</u> dogs like chewing on bones.

However, when we are talking about members of a specific group, we add "of the" after the quantifier. For example:

Few of the cats in my neighborhood like water.

All of the dogs got some bones to chew on.

Both, either and neither

We use the quantifiers "both", "either" and "neither" when we are talking about two people or things. The quantifier "both" takes the plural form of the verb while the quantifiers "either" and "neither" take the singular form. For example:

One girl	Two girls	More than two girls
Each girl is wearing a blue dress.	Both the girls are wearing blue dresses.	All of the girls are wearing blue dresses.
Every girl is not wearing a blue dress.	Neither of the girls is wearing a blue dress.	None of the girls are wearing a blue dress.
I don't think every girl owns a blue dress.	I don't think either of the girls owns a blue dress.	I don't think any of the girls own a blue dress.

Exercise 28

In each of the following sentences, choose the correct quantifier from the choices in brackets:

1. I have (some; none; few) money in my pocket.

2. Tanya does not like (many, much) spicy food.

3. The teacher gave (each; both; all) child a book.

4. The twins do not play basketball because (either; neither; none; all) of them is very good at sports.

5. (All; All of the) children like stories but (few; few of the) children in my little sister's class know how to read.

Lesson 20: Possessives

Like demonstratives, possessives can be a kind of pronoun. In Chapter 3 we discussed the possessive pronouns, such as "mine", "yours" "his", "hers", "its", "ours" and "theirs".

The possessive determiners also show possession but unlike possessive pronouns, they cannot stand alone. They have to go together with a noun. These are the possessive determiners:

		Singular	**Plural**
		Possessive pronoun	**Possessive pronoun**
First person		my	our
Second person		your	your
Third person			their
	Male	his	
	Female	her	
	Neuter	its	

Here are examples of how we use these possessive determiners in sentences, with the possessive determiners underlined:

The book belongs to me. It is <u>my</u> book.
The book belongs to you. It is <u>your</u> book.
The book belongs to him. It is <u>his</u> book.
The book belongs to her. It is <u>her</u> book.
The book belongs to it. It is <u>its</u> book.
The book belongs to us. It is <u>our</u> book.
The book belongs to you. It is <u>your</u> book.
The book belongs to them. It is <u>their</u> book.

Exercise 29

Replace the possessive nouns in brackets with the appropriate possessive determiners. For example:

Patricia is taking care of (Tim's) dog.

Patricia is taking care of <u>his</u> dog.

1. Peter works at the zoo, where (Peter's) job is to take care of the animals.

2. Manuela has opened (Manuela's) own nail salon in New York.

3. Tokyo is the largest city in the world. (Tokyo's) population is 37.8 million.

4. Simon and Joanne, bring in (Simon's and Joanne's) toys!

5. Jean has two goldfish. (The goldfish's) names are Tom and Jerry.

Chapter 5: Verbs and verb tenses

Verbs are "doing" words. We use them to describe an action, something that happens or a state of being.

Lesson 21: Action verbs and stative verbs

We can group verbs into action verbs and stative verbs.

Action verbs

Action verbs, like the name suggests, are verbs that describe an action. We can also call them dynamic verbs because they describe activities and processes, as well as physical conditions.

Examples of action verbs are: sing, speak, grow, change, itch, ache, hit, melt, read, watch, go.

We can use these verbs in their continuous form to describe a continuous action. (We will discuss the continuous forms verbs later on in this chapter.)

For example:

> My belly is aching.
>
> We were dancing until dawn.
>
> She will be speaking at tonight's function.

Stative verbs

Stative verbs, also called state verbs, usually describe conditions that are more static. They describe emotions, states of being, understanding and perception of the senses.

Examples of stative verbs are: be, feel, love, like, appear, wish, want, own, owe, resemble, understand, suspect, believe, mean, hear.

We do not usually use stative verbs in their continuous form. When we do, it is to show that the state they describe is more of an action at that moment.

For example:

Nick <u>is</u> rude. (In this sentence, we are saying that Nick is a rude person all of the time.)

Nick <u>is being</u> rude. (In this sentence, we are saying that Nick is not always rude but right now he is doing something that makes him rude.)

Sometimes when we use the stative verb in the continuous form, it changes the verb's meaning completely. For example:

Stative meaning	Active meaning
She <u>looks</u> great in that outfit. (She appears great.)	She <u>is looking</u> at the dress in the shop window. (She is directing her eyes towards the dress.)
Jack <u>has</u> a bicycle. (Jack owns a bicycle.)	Jack <u>is having</u> dinner. (Jack is eating dinner.)
Susan <u>sees</u> John. (Susan notices John.)	Susan <u>is seeing</u> John. (Susan is dating John.)

This chocolate <u>tastes</u> great. (The chocolate has a great taste.)	I <u>am tasting</u> the chocolate. (I am testing the chocolate.)
I <u>expect</u> that Mike will be tired after his trip. (I assume that Mike will be tired.)	I <u>am expecting</u> Mike at eight. (I am waiting for Mike to arrive at eight.)

When we use the stative verbs in a way that gives them an active meaning, we can also use them in the simple form. For example:

The chef <u>tastes</u> the sauce.

Exercise 30

Identify the verbs in these sentences and say whether they are action verbs or stative verbs:

1. I love my new puppy.

2. The boys are fishing in the river.

3. Cynthia drinks tea but right now she is drinking coffee.

4. How are you feeling?

5. The shopkeeper weighs the potatoes. They weigh two pounds.

Lesson 22: Transitive verbs and intransitive verbs

Verbs can be transitive or they can be intransitive.

Transitive verbs

When a verb is transitive, it goes with a direct object. For example:

The dog <u>eats</u> *its food.*

Mindy <u>loves</u> *Luke.*

Shelley <u>brings</u> *her teacher* some flowers.

In all three of these examples, there is a direct object: "its food", "Luke" and "her teacher" respectively. These direct objects receive the action from the verbs that go before them. Transitive verbs are usually action verbs.

Intransitive verbs

Intransitive verbs do not need a direct object to still show their meaning. For example:

The girl <u>sings</u>.

The dog <u>eats</u>.

We do not need to know what the girl is singing or what the dog is eating to understand what they are doing.

Even though intransitive verbs do not need a direct object, they often go together with an adjective, an adverb, a preposition or a verb complement such as an infinitive.

Here are some examples:

The water is cold. (The word "cold" is an adjective, which we discuss in Chapter 6.)

The girl sings beautifully. (The word "beautifully" is an adverb, which we discuss in Chapter 7.)

The dog eats in the kitchen. (The phrase "in the kitchen" is a preposition of place, which we discuss in Chapter 8.)

Kathy loves to cook food for her family. (The phrase "to cook" is an infinitive, which we discuss in Lesson 24.)

Exercise 31

Identify the verbs in these sentences and say whether they are transitive or intransitive verbs:

1. The player hits the ball.
2. The spectators cheer happily.
3. Gerald buys a hot dog from the vendor.
4. The hot dog tastes delicious.
5. Sylvia does not like hot dogs.
6. She prefers eating French fries.
7. Cindy prefers French fries too.
8. Jim is watching the game.
9. Lynn is watching on television.
10. We all love to see our team in action.

Lesson 23: The present, past and past participle forms of verbs

Most verbs change form depending on whether they show an action in the present or the past. There are three forms: the present or base form of the verb, the past form and the past participle. We will discuss later on in this chapter how to use these forms to make different tenses.

In terms of how they change form, we can group verbs into regular verbs and irregular verbs.

Regular verbs

Regular verbs change form in the same way. For the past and past participle forms, we take the present form of the verb and simply add –ed at the end. For example:

Present	**Past**	**Past participle**
watch	watch**ed**	watch**ed**
pack	pack**ed**	pack**ed**
cook	cook**ed**	cook**ed**
spray	spray**ed**	spray**ed**
ski	ski**ed**	ski**ed**
echo	echo**ed**	echo**ed**

Some regular verbs form their past and past participle forms in slightly different ways:

- When the regular verb ends with –e, we just add –d. For example:

Present	Past	Past participle
free	free**d**	free**d**
live	live**d**	live**d**
tie	tie**d**	tie**d**

- When the regular verb ends with a consonant followed directly by –y, we change the –y to –I and add –ed. For example:

Present	Past	Past participle
dirty	dirt**ied**	dirt**ied**
cry	cried	cried
ply	plied	plied

- When the regular verb ends with a consonant followed directly by a vowel and another consonant and the stress is on the last syllable of the word, we double the final consonant and add –ed. For example:

Present	Past	Past participle
beg	beg**ged**	beg**ged**
hop	hop**ped**	hop**ped**
regret	regret**ted**	regret**ted**
compel	compel**led**	compel**led**

Note: In US English, we do not double the final consonant when the stress is not on the last syllable of the word. However, in UK English we do sometimes double the final consonant. For example:

Present	Past	Past participle
travel	travel**ed** (US English) travelled (UK English)	travel**ed** (US English) travelled (UK English)

The best way to be sure is to use a good dictionary.

Irregular verbs

Irregular verbs either change form completely in the past or past participle forms or they do not change at all. Sometimes the way they change depends on regional differences or it depends on how we use the word. Sometimes there are two possibilities and both are correct!

The following is a list of some irregular verbs in English:

Present	Past	Past participle
arise	arose	arisen
awake	awoke	awoken; awakened
bear	bore	bore
beat	beat	beaten; beat
become	became	become
befall	befell	befallen
begin	began	begun
behold	beheld	beheld
bend	bent	bent
beset	beset	beset
bet	bet	bet

bid	bid	bid
bind	bound	bound
bite	bit	bitten
bleed	bled	bled
blow	blew	blown
break	broke	broken
breed	bred	bred
bring	brought	brought
build	built	built
burn	burned (US English) burnt (UK English)	burned (US English) burnt (UK English)
burst	burst	burst
buy	bought	bought
cast	cast	cast
catch	caught	caught
choose	chose	chosen
cling	clung	clung
come	came	come
cost	cost	cost
creep	crept	crept
cut	cut	cut
deal	dealt	dealt
dig	dug	dug
do	did	done
draw	drew	drawn

dream	dreamed (while sleeping) dreamt (hope for or imagine)	dreamed (while sleeping) dreamt (hope for or imagine)
drink	drank	drunk
drive	drove	driven
eat	ate	eaten
fall	fell	fallen
feed	fed	fed
feel	felt	felt
fight	fought	fought
find	found	found
flee	fled	fled
fling	flung	flung
fly	flew	flown
forbid	forbade	forbidden
forecast	forecast	forecast
forego	forewent	foregone
foresee	foresaw	foreseen
foretell	foretold	foretold
forget	forgot	forgotten forgot (in some parts of the USA)
freeze	froze	frozen
get	got	gotten (in US and Canadian English) got

give	gave	given
go	went	gone
grind	ground	ground
grow	grew	grown
hang	hung (hang something) hanged (death by hanging)	hung (hang something) hanged (death by hanging)
have	had	had
hear	heard	heard
hide	hid	hidden
hit	hit	hit
hold	held	held
hurt	hurt	hurt
keep	kept	kept
kneel	knelt; kneeled	knelt; kneeled
know	knew	known
lay	laid	laid
lead	led	led
lean	leaned	Leaned
leap	leaped (mainly US English) leapt (mainly UK English)	leaped (mainly US English) leapt (mainly UK English)
learn	learned learnt (mainly UK English)	learned learnt (mainly UK English)

leave	left	left
lend	lent	lent
let	let	let
lie	lay	lain
light	lit	lit
lose	lost	lost
make	made	made
mean	meant	meant
meet	met	met
mow	mowed	mowed; mown
pay	paid	paid
put	put	put
quit	quit	quit
read	read	read
rend	rent	rent
rid	rid	rid
ride	rode	ridden
ring	rang	rung
rise	rose	risen
run	ran	run
saw	sawed	sawed (mainly US and Canadian English) sawn
say	said	said

see	saw	seen
seek	sought	sought
sell	sold	sold
send	sent	sent
set	set	set
shake	shook	shaken
shear	sheared	sheared; shorn
shed	shed	shed
shine	shone (emitting light) shined (polishing)	shone (emitting light) shined (polishing)
shoot	shot	shot
show	showed	shown; showed
shrink	shrank	shrunk
shut	shut	shut
sing	sang	sung
sink	sank	sunk
sit	sat	sat
slay	slew	slain
sleep	slept	slept
slide	slid	slid
sling	slung	slung
smell	smelled smelt (mainly UK English)	smelled smelt (mainly UK English)
sow	sowed	sown, sowed

speak	spoke	spoken
speed	sped	sped
spend	spent	spent
spin	spun	spun
spit	spat	spat
split	split	split
spread	spread	spread
spring	sprang; sprung	sprung
stand	stood	stood
steal	stole	stolen
stick	stuck	stuck
stink	stank	stunk
stride	strode	stridden
strike	struck	struck
swear	swore	sworn
sweep	swept	swept
swell	swelled	swollen
swim	swam	swum
swing	swung	swung
take	took	taken
teach	taught	taught
tear	tore	torn
tell	told	told
think	thought	thought
throw	threw	thrown

thrust	thrust	thrust
tread	trod	trodden trod (mainly US and Australian English)
wake	woke	woken
wear	wore	worn
weave	wove weaved (moving from side to side through a crowd)	wove weaved (moving from side to side through a crowd)
weep	wept	wept
win	won	won
wind	wound	wound
withdraw	withdrew	withdrawn
withhold	withheld	withheld
withstand	withstood	withstood
wring	wrung	wrung
write	wrote	written

Exercise 32

Give the past and past participle forms of these verbs:

1. begin
2. eat
3. love
4. rely
5. repel
6. repeal
7. throw
8. set
9. boggle
10. run

Lesson 24: The infinitive

When we look up a verb in the dictionary, we use the verb's present tense or base form. We can also call this the verb's bare infinitive.

Another form of the verb is its full infinitive. In English, we form the full infinitive simply by adding the word "to" in front of the base form. For example: to eat, to sleep, to learn.

When it is part of an infinitive, the word "to" is not a preposition. Instead, it is part of the verb. The base form of the verb does not change in any way either. For example, look at the difference between these sentences:

Kali would like to go to Paris one day.

Here we use the infinitive "to go" after the verb "like".

She is looking forward to going to Paris.

Here the word "to" is a preposition and "going" is a present participle, which we will discuss later on.

We can use the infinitive in different ways:

- The infinitive can be the subject of a sentence. For example:

    To sing is one of the greatest joys in life.

- We can use the infinitive like an adjective or adverb phrase, usually to express intent or desire. For example:

    Their orders are to march to the next town.

- We often use the infinitive directly after an indirect object. For example:

  Chester asked Jane <u>to meet</u> him at the coffee shop.

- The infinitive often follows certain verbs, such as: agree, plan, try, expect, need, mean, pretend, offer, begin, promise, use, want, would like, love.

Exercise 33

Identify and underline the full infinitives in this paragraph:

Doron asked Rachel <u>to marry</u> him last month. They plan <u>to have</u> their wedding in July. Rachel would like a small wedding with only a few guests but Doron wants all their friends and family <u>to come</u>. This is not the only thing that they disagree on. For instance, Rachel would love <u>to have</u> a chocolate wedding cake while Doron would prefer <u>to have</u> a vanilla cake instead. Luckily they have learned that <u>to compromise</u> is one of the most important ingredients for a successful marriage. They will have <u>to work</u> through their differences and find a solution that will work for both of them. At least they are both looking forward to being partners for the rest of their lives.

Lesson 25: Verb conjugation

When a verb changes form, for instance from its base form to the past tense, we say that we conjugate that verb. A conjugated verb can communicate the tense. For example, when we see the verb "ate", we know that it indicates that the subject has eaten in the past.

In English, verbs also conjugate according to the subject. We call this subject–verb agreement. In the simple present tense, we add an –s to the verb when the subject is the third person singular:

Singular		Plural	
First person	I <u>eat</u>.	First person	We <u>eat</u>.
Second person	You <u>eat</u>.	Second person	You <u>eat</u>.
Third person	He <u>eats</u>. She <u>eats</u>. It <u>eats</u>.	Third person	They <u>eat</u>.

The verbs "be", "have" and "do" conjugate differently in the simple present tense:

- be

Singular		Plural	
First person	I <u>am</u>.	First person	We <u>are</u>.
Second person	You <u>are</u>.	Second person	You <u>are</u>.
Third person	He <u>is</u>. She <u>is</u>. It <u>is</u>.	Third person	They <u>are</u>.

- have

Singular		Plural	
First person	I <u>have</u>.	First person	We <u>have</u>.
Second person	You <u>have</u>.	Second person	You <u>have</u>.
Third person	He <u>has</u>. She <u>has</u>. It <u>has</u>.	Third person	They <u>have</u>.

- do

Singular		Plural	
First person	I <u>do</u>.	First person	We <u>do</u>.
Second person	You <u>do</u>.	Second person	You <u>do</u>.
Third person	He <u>does</u>. She <u>does</u>. It <u>does</u>.	Third person	They <u>do</u>.

In the simple past tense, the verb takes the same form for everybody. For example:

Singular		Plural	
First person	I <u>ate</u>.	First person	We <u>ate</u>.
Second person	You <u>ate</u>.	Second person	You <u>ate</u>.
Third person	He <u>ate</u>. She <u>ate</u>. It <u>ate</u>.	Third person	They <u>ate</u>.

The only exception is the past tense of the verb "be":

Singular		Plural	
First person	I was.	First person	We were.
Second person	You were.	Second person	You were.
Third person	He was. She was. It was.	Third person	They were.

When we use a verb, we should always check that the form of the verb agrees with the subject.

Exercise 34

Fill in the correct form of the verb in brackets in each of these sentences:

1. John and Mary _____ (go) to work at seven in the morning while Peter _____ (go) to work at eight.

2. _____ (Do) Gina like broccoli?

3. I _____ (be) so excited about the concert next Friday! Danny _____ (be) in the band and they _____ (be) very good.

4. Sean _____ (have) a cold. He _____ (have) a cold last winter too.

5. Mark _____ (be) late for class last Monday but we _____ (be) on time.

Lesson 26: The –ing form of verbs

One of the ways that we conjugate verbs is to the –ing form of the verb. As the name implies, the –ing form is the verb with –ing added. For example: jump**ing**, sleep**ing**, bark**ing**, ski**ing**.

For some verbs, we form the –ing form in a different way:

- When the base form of the verb ends on a silent e or an ue, we take away the e before adding –ing. For example:

Base form	–ing form
love	lov**ing**
debate	debat**ing**
hope	hop**ing**
glue	glu**ing**
accrue	accru**ing**

An exception is the word "dye", where we just add the –ing: dye**ing**.

- When the base form of the verb ends in –ie, we change the ie to y and then add –ing. For example:

Base form	–ing form
lie	lying
tie	tying
vie	vying
die	dying

- When the verb ends in a vowel and one consonant, we double that consonant and then add –ing. For example:

Base form	–ing form
hop	hopping
pat	patting
beg	begging
rig	rigging
put	putting

- When the base form of the verb ends in a stressed vowel and an r, we double the r and then add –ing. For example:

Base form	–ing form
deter	deter**ring**
refer	refer**ring**
concur	concur**ring**

- When the base form of the verb ends in an unstressed vowel and an r, we only add –ing. For example:

Base form	–ing form
answer	answer**ing**
mutter	mutter**ing**
offer	offer**ing**

We can use the –ing form as a present participle or as a gerund.

The present participle

We use the present participle in different ways:

- As part of the continuous form: To indicate the continuous tense, we use the present participle along with a helping verb. (We will discuss helping verbs and the continuous tenses later on in this chapter.) For example:

    He is <u>going</u> to college next year. (The helping verb is "is".)

- After verbs of perception: We can use a verb of perception, such as "see", "hear" or "feel", along with the object and the present participle. For example:

    The tourists see a shark <u>swimming</u> in the ocean. (The verb of perception is "see"; the object is "a shark".)

- After verbs of action: We can use the present participle after a verb of movement, action or position to show that two activities are happening at the same time. For example:

    I jog <u>listening</u> to music. (The verb "jog" is a verb of action. I jog and listen to music at the same time.)

- As an adjective: We can use the present participle as an adjective to describe a noun or pronoun. For example:

    This class is <u>exciting</u>.

The gerund

The gerund looks exactly like the present participle but it is not a verb. Instead, we use the gerund as a noun. For example:

His <u>singing</u> is terrible.
She is good at <u>knitting</u>.
I enjoy <u>walking</u>.

Exercise 35

Give the –ing form of each of these verbs:

1. howl
2. spy
3. shop
4. cope
5. belie
6. occur
7. pamper
8. die
9. dye
10. argue

Lesson 27: Auxiliary verbs

Auxiliary verbs are helping verbs. We can use an auxiliary verb together with the main verb. There are three reasons why we do this:

1. To show the main verb's tense, for example: I <u>have eaten</u> already. I <u>am feeling</u> full now.

2. To form a negative, for example: I <u>do not want</u> another portion.

3. To form a question, for example: <u>Do</u> you <u>want</u> another portion?

The main auxiliary verbs are "have", "do" and "be" in their different forms. However, these verbs are not always auxiliary verbs. For example:

Sandra <u>has</u> bought a new book. (The verb "has" is an auxiliary verb to show the tense of the main verb "buy".)

Sandra now <u>has</u> five hundred books. (The verb "has" is an action verb.)

<u>Does</u> Sandra like to read? (The verb "does" is an auxiliary verb to form a question with the main verb "like".)

Sandra <u>does</u> crossword puzzles too. (The verb "does" is an action verb.)

Sandra <u>is</u> reading her new book. (The verb "is" is an auxiliary verb to show the tense of the main verb "read".)

Sandra <u>is</u> a bookworm. (The verb "is" is a linking verb.)

Exercise 36

Underline the auxiliary verbs in this paragraph:

Uncle Jim and Aunt Sally have three children. Peter, the eldest, <u>is</u> working with Doctors Without Borders in the Middle East. Paul is the middle child and he <u>is</u> studying. He <u>does</u> not want to become a doctor like his brother but instead he <u>is</u> studying to become a teacher. What <u>does</u> the youngest, Mary, do? She <u>has</u> finished high school and <u>has</u> joined the military.

Lesson 28: Modal verbs

Modal verbs are similar to auxiliary verbs in that they are helping verbs. We use modal verbs to express ability, obligation or intent, possibility or permission. Sometimes the modal verb goes with the word "to" and then we call it a modal phrase.

The modal verbs and phrases in English are: can, could, be able to, may, might, shall, should, ought to, must, have to, will, would. We use each of these modal verbs with the base form of the verb.

Can/could/be able to

We use the modal verbs "can" and its past tense "could" and the modal phrase "be able to" to express ability or the lack of ability. For example:

<u>Can</u> Jack fly? No, Jack <u>cannot</u> fly but he <u>can</u> run very fast.

Jack <u>could</u> run fast even when he was a boy.

I would love to <u>be able to</u> run as fast as Jack.

We can also use these verbs to express other things:

- Possibility or impossibility:

    Jack <u>could</u> fly if he had wings.

- Asking or giving permission:

    <u>Can</u> I go running with Jack tomorrow?

    Yes, you <u>can</u> if he agrees to it.

- Making a suggestion:

    Maybe you <u>could</u> run with Jack next weekend too.

May/might

We use "may" mainly to ask for or give permission. For example:

Jack says that I <u>may</u> run with him tomorrow.

We also use "may" for polite requests. For example:

<u>May</u> I help you?

We use "might" for a polite suggestion. For example:

Jack, you <u>might</u> like to try these new running shoes.

We can use both "may" or "might" to express a possibility or impossibility. For example:

Jack and I <u>may</u> run in a race next month.

We <u>might not</u> do well in the race if we do not train properly.

Another use for "may" and "might" is to make a suggestion where there is no better alternative. When we use these modal verbs in this way, we add "as well" to turn them into modal phrases. For example:

We <u>may as well</u> go running while the sun is shining.

I <u>might as well</u> go running with Jack. I do not have any other plans.

Shall/should/ought to

The modal verbs "shall", "should" and "ought to" are verbs that we use when we are being polite.

We use "shall" for offering assistance or for suggesting something, especially when we think that the answer may be positive. However, we use this modal verb only with "I" and "we". For example:

>Shall I help you find your running shoes?

>Shall we run?

We can use "should" in a similar way to "shall", to offer assistance or to suggest something. For example:

>Should I give you some water?

>Should we go running in the morning?

Another use for "should" is to predict something. For example:

>We should be back by eight if we go running early in the morning.

>It should not take a long time to go for a run.

We can also use "should" and "ought to" when we want to give advice. For example:

>You should bring a water bottle on your run.

>You should not run the race in brand new shoes.

>We ought to go to bed early on the night before the race.

Must/have to/need to

We use the modal verbs "must" and "have to" to describe something that is supposed to happen or to persuade someone to do something. For example:

You <u>must</u> have a race number to participate in the race.

To get your race number, you <u>have to</u> fill in an entry form.

You <u>must</u> try running this race at least once!

You <u>have to</u> experience the camaraderie among the runners.

We can also use "must" to express an opinion that is quite certainly true. For example:

Shane has run the race many times. He <u>must</u> love it.

When we want to describe something that should not happen or that is not allowed, we use the negative forms "must not". For example:

You <u>must not</u> miss the deadline for sending in your entry.

For something that is not really necessary, we use "do not have to". For example:

We <u>do not have to</u> be experienced runners to participate in the race.

Shane has run the race so often that they send him an entry form every year. He <u>does not have</u> to ask for one.

We use "need to" in similar ways as "have to" but normally we use it for something that is less urgent. For example:

We <u>need to</u> try and get there early on race day.

When we use "need to" for making a suggestion, its negative form is "need not", without the word "to". For example:

Shane <u>need not</u> worry that we will run faster than him because he is a much better runner than us.

Will/would

We use the modal verb "will" to express the future tenses, which we will discuss in Lessons 29, 30, 31 and 32.

However, we can also use "will" for a polite request. For example:

<u>Will</u> you pick us up after the race, please?

We can use "would" for a polite request too. For example:

<u>Would</u> you come support us on race day?

<u>Would</u> you mind taking some photographs of us?

Another way to use "would" is to express a wish or desire. For example:

I <u>would</u> love to do well in the race.

I <u>would not</u> like to come in last place.

We also use "would" to describe a habit that took place in the past. For example:

When I was a child, I <u>would</u> spend hours reading. I <u>would not</u> go for a run just for the fun of it.

Exercise 37

Choose the most appropriate modal verb from the options in brackets.

As a little girl, Diana _____ (would, might, ought to) dream of becoming a ballerina. Now that she is all grown up, she knows that she _____ (is able to, ought to, would) focus on other dreams instead. She is too clumsy to be a graceful dancer but she _____ (can, must, may) sing beautifully. She _____ (shall, should, would) enter that talent competition on television. After all, she _____ (must, needs to, could) do very well.

Lesson 29: The simple verb tenses

We use verb tenses to show when an action happens. The simple verb tenses are for describing actions without saying whether these actions are completed or whether they are still happening.

Resources:

For an easy-to-understand chart showing the simple verb tenses, see http://www.eslcharts.com/verb-tenses-chart.html.

Follow this link for an animated presentation of the verb tenses: http://www.elihinkel.org/tips/tenses.htm

The simple present tense

We use the simple present tense for different reasons:

- To describe a fact or a habit. For example:

    Dee <u>loves</u> dogs.

    Dee <u>walks</u> her dog every day.

- To describe something that will happen in future but that happens at regular or scheduled times. For example:

    The sun <u>rises</u> at 5:30 in the morning.

    Jake's band <u>plays</u> next Tuesday night.

- To tell a story or a joke. For example:

    A horse <u>walks</u> into a bar and the barman <u>asks</u>, "Why the long face?"

To form the simple present tense, we use the base form of the verb, as discussed in Lesson 23, and conjugate it, as discussed in Lesson 25.

- For the third person singular, we add an –s to the verb. For example:

  He eat**s**. She eat**s**. It eat**s**.

- For everyone else, we simply use the base form of the verb. For example: I eat. You eat. We eat. They eat.

To form a question in the simple present tense, we use "do" or "does" with the base form of the verb. For example:

Do you like cats?

Does Mary like cats?

To form a negative in the simple present tense, we use "do not" or "does not" with the base form of the verb. For example:

I do not like spiders.

Karla does not like spiders either.

To form questions and negatives with the verb "be" in the simple present tense, we do not use "do" or "does".

- For questions, we conjugate the verb "be" and then place it at the beginning of the question. For example:

  Am I scared of spiders?

  Are you scared of spiders?

  Is Karla scared of spiders?

- For negatives, we conjugate the verb "be" and add the word "not". For example:

    I <u>am not</u> scared of spiders.

    Karla <u>is not</u> scared of spiders either.

    We <u>are not</u> scared of spiders at all.

The simple past tense

We use the simple past tense to describe an activity that started and ended in the past.

To form the simple past tense, we simply use the past tense form of the verb, as discussed in Lesson 23. For example:

   Daniel <u>lived</u> in Kenya when he <u>was</u> a child.

   I <u>saw</u> a movie about Kenya last week.

To form a question in the simple past tense, we use the past form of "do" or "does", which is "did", along with the base form of the verb. For example:

   <u>Did</u> Daniel <u>live</u> on a farm in Kenya?

   <u>Did</u> you <u>see</u> the movie about Kenya?

To form a negative in the simple past tense, we use "did not" along with the base form of the verb. For example:

   Daniel <u>did not live</u> on a farm.

   Peter and Annie <u>did not see</u> the movie about Kenya.

To form questions and negatives with the verb "be" in the simple past tense, we do not use "did".

- For questions, we conjugate the verb "be" in its past form and then place it at the beginning of the question. For example:

    <u>Was</u> Daniel happy in Kenya?

    <u>Were</u> Peter and Annie at the movies last Tuesday?

- For negatives, we conjugate the verb "be" in its past form and add the word "not". For example:

    Daniel <u>was not</u> unhappy in Kenya.

    Peter and Annie <u>were not</u> at the movies last Tuesday.

The simple future tense

We use the simple future tense to describe an activity that will happen in the future.

To form the simple future tense, we use the modal verb "will" along with the base form of the verb. For example:

  I <u>will go</u> to the clinic tomorrow.

  The doctor <u>will examine</u> me.

To form a question in the simple future tense, we use "will" and the base form of the verb but we change the word order. For example:

  <u>Will</u> you <u>come</u> to the clinic with me?

  <u>Will</u> the doctor <u>check</u> my blood pressure?

To form a negative in the simple future tense, we use "will not" and the base form of the verb. For example:

  I <u>will not be</u> scared.

  The doctor <u>will not give</u> me an injection.

Exercise 38

Fill in the correct form of the words in brackets in each of these sentences:

1. I _____ (be) scared of snakes.

2. Last year a snake _____ (bite) me.

3. The snake that _____ (bite) me last year _____ (be) small. Its bite _____ (hurt) at all.

4. Tomorrow in the woods I _____ (take) a big stick with me to chase away snakes.

5. _____ (remember) (you) to wear sturdy shoes on our hike in the woods tomorrow?

Lesson 30: The progressive verb tenses

The progressive tenses are also called the continuous tenses. We use them to describe ongoing actions, or actions in progress.

Resources:

For an easy-to-understand chart showing the progressive verb tenses, see http://www.eslcharts.com/verb-tenses-chart.html.

Follow this link for an animated presentation of the verb tenses: http://www.elihinkel.org/tips/tenses.htm

The present progressive tense

We use the present progressive tense to describe an action that is happening now and has not ended yet.

To form the present progressive tense, we use the verb "be" in its conjugated form, as discussed in Lesson 25, along with the present participle of the verb that describes the action, as discussed in Lesson 26. For example:

> I am opening the front gate.
>
> It is raining.
>
> I must get inside because my clothes are getting wet.

To form a question in the present progressive tense, we use the conjugated form of "be" and the present participle of the main verb but we change the order. For example:

> Am I running fast enough?
>
> Are you unlocking the door?
>
> Is the rain falling hard?

To form a negative in the present progressive tense, we use the conjugated form of "be" along with "not" and the present participle of the main verb. For example:

I <u>am not running</u> fast enough to get out of the rain.

The rain <u>is not falling</u> very hard right now.

We are not getting too wet.

The past progressive tense

We use the past progressive tense to describe an action that was happening at a certain point in the past.

To form the past progressive tense, we use the past form of "be", together with the present participle of the main verb. For example:

It <u>was raining</u> when I got home from work yesterday.

The dogs <u>were barking</u> as I opened the front door.

When we want to form a question in the past progressive tense, we use the past form of "be" and the present participle of the main verb but we change the word order. For example:

<u>Was</u> it <u>raining</u> when you left the house this morning?

<u>Were</u> the dogs <u>barking</u> last night when you arrived home?

To form a negative in the past progressive tense, we use the past form of "be" along with "not" and the present participle of the main verb. For example:

It <u>was not raining</u> when I left the house this morning.

The dogs <u>were not barking</u> at seven last night.

The future progressive tense

We use the future progressive tense to describe an action that will be in progress at some point in the future.

To form the future progressive tense, we use the modal verb "will" along with the verb "be" and the present participle of the main verb. For example:

>I think it <u>will be raining</u> when I come home tonight.

>The dogs <u>will be barking</u> as I open the front door tonight.

To form a question in the future progressive tense, we use the modal verb "will" along with the verb "be" and the present participle of the main verb but we change the word order. For example:

><u>Will</u> it <u>be raining</u> when we leave for work tomorrow?

><u>Will</u> the dogs <u>be barking</u> as you arrive home tonight?

Exercise 39

Fill in the correct form of the words in brackets in each of these sentences:

1. Andy and Chris _____ (plan) their next big trip.

2. _____ (visit) (they) Mexico when we arrive in Acapulco?

3. I _____ (eat) breakfast when my aunt arrived this morning.

4. My aunt _____ (not carry) an umbrella even though it _____ (rain).

5. It looks as if the sun _____ (shine) when the match starts this afternoon.

Lesson 31: The perfect verb tenses

We normally use the perfect tenses to describe an action in the past.

Resources:

For an easy-to-understand chart showing the perfect verb tenses, see http://www.eslcharts.com/verb-tenses-chart.html.

Follow this link for an animated presentation of the verb tenses: http://www.elihinkel.org/tips/tenses.htm

The present perfect tense

We use the present perfect tense for different types of actions:

- An action that happened at some time in the past: We do not need to know exactly when the action happened. For example:

    I <u>have</u> already <u>eaten</u>.

    Tom <u>has visited</u> Nigeria.

    When there is a time word such as "yesterday", "a month ago" or "last week", we use the simple past tense. For example:

    I <u>ate</u> yesterday.

    Tom <u>visited</u> Nigeria last year.

- An action that happened in the past but has an effect on the present moment, for example:

    I <u>have finished</u> my work, so I can relax now.

    John <u>has been</u> ill, so he is behind with his lessons.

- An action that started in the past and is still happening, for example:

    You <u>have been</u> a great friend to me. (You started being a great friend to me in the past and you are still a great friend to me.)

    Sean's father <u>has worked</u> for the same company for 20 years. (Sean's father started working for the company 20 years ago and is still working for them.)

Time words that often go with the present perfect tense are "since" and "for". For example:

   Gina <u>has been</u> a singer **since** 2006.

   Gina <u>has been</u> a singer **for** 10 years.

Other expressions of time that we use with the present perfect tense include: already, yet, recently, ever, before, lately, just, at last.

To form the present perfect tense, we use the auxiliary verb "have" in its conjugated form, along with the past participle of the main verb, which we discussed in Lesson 23.

When we want to form a question in the present perfect tense, we change the word order so that the question begins with "have" in its conjugated form. For example:

   <u>Have</u> you ever <u>been</u> to Nigeria?

   <u>Has</u> the dog <u>eaten</u> yet?

To form a negative in the present perfect tense, we simple add "not" after "have" in its conjugated form, and then add the past participle of the main verb. For example:

I have not been to Nigeria.

The dog has not eaten yet.

The time word "never" often goes with the present perfect tense but because it is a negative expression already, we do not use "not" along with it. For example:

I <u>have never been</u> to Nigeria.

It is incorrect to say:

I have not never been to Nigeria.

The past perfect tense

We use the past perfect tense mainly to describe an action that finished before another action in the past, for example:

Before we had dinner, John <u>had</u> already <u>eaten</u> a bag of crisps.

When they started their band, Eddie and Paul <u>had been</u> friends for five years already.

To form the past perfect tense, we use the past form of the auxiliary verb "have", which is "had", along with the past participle of the main verb.

To form a question in the past perfect tense, we change the word order to start the sentence with "had". For example:

<u>Had</u> Mary <u>eaten</u> anything before dinner?

We form a negative in the past perfect tense by adding "not" after "had" and then using the past participle of the main verb too. For example:

Mary <u>had not eaten</u> anything before dinner.

The future perfect tense

There are three ways in which we can use the future perfect tense:

- To describe an action that will be completed before a specific time in the future, for example:

  John will have eaten a bag of crisps by dinner time.

- To describe an action that will still be happening at a specific time in the future, for example:

  Next year you and I will have been friends for 20 years.

- To describe an action that has happened for certain in the near past. We normally use a time expression such as "by now" a case like this. For example:

  Tom's airplane to Nigeria will have left by now.

The future perfect tense often goes with time expressions such as: before, by, by the time, until.

To form the future perfect tense, we use the modal verb "will" along with "have" and the past participle of the main verb. We can also say that we use "will" with the present perfect form.

When we want to ask a question in the future perfect tense, we change the word order to start the question with "will". For example:

  Will Mary have eaten yet by 7 o'clock?

For the negative form of the future perfect tense, we add "not" after "will" and then add "have" and the past participle of the main verb. For example:

  Mary will not have eaten by 7 o'clock.

Exercise 40

Fill in the correct form of the words in brackets in the following sentences:

1. A new Indian restaurant _____ (open) down the street recently.

2. Last night we went for a meal at the new restaurant but Jimmy _____ (had) a big lunch already.

3. _____ (eat) (you) (ever) a real Indian curry?

4. Susan _____ (like) (never) spicy food but she loves the chicken tikka masala.

5. We will go to the restaurant again on Friday night and hopefully Jimmy _____ (remember) not to eat too much for lunch.

Lesson 32: The perfect progressive verb tenses

The perfect progressive verb tenses, also called the perfect continuous tenses, are a combination of the perfect and progressive tenses. We use them to describe continuing actions that started in the past.

Resources:

For an easy-to-understand chart showing the perfect progressive verb tenses, see http://www.eslcharts.com/verb-tenses-chart.html.

Follow this link for an animated presentation of the verb tenses: http://www.elihinkel.org/tips/tenses.htm

The present perfect progressive tense

We use the present perfect progressive tense for different kinds of actions:

- Actions that have started in the past and are still happening, for example:

    The loud music <u>has been playing</u> for three hours now. I wish it would stop.

    Ellen and Diana <u>have been working</u> in the restaurant since 2010. They are still working there.

- Actions that happened in the past and have ended recently, for example:

    I <u>have been waiting</u> here since noon. I'm glad you have finally arrived.

    The band <u>has been playing</u> all night. They are taking a break now.

Like with the present perfect tense, we often use the time words "for" or "since" with the present perfect progressive tense.

To form the present perfect progressive tense, we use the auxiliary verb "have" in its conjugated form, along with "been" – the past participle of "be" – and the present participle of the main verb.

When we want to form a question in the present perfect progressive tense, we change the word order to start the question with the conjugated form of "have". For example:

>Have you been waiting long?

>Has Thelma been crying?

We form the negative in the present perfect progressive tense by adding "not" after the conjugated form of "have". For example:

>I have not been waiting long.

>Thelma has not been crying.

The past perfect progressive tense

We use the past perfect progressive tense to describe an action that had been going on until a certain point in the past. For example:

>Angie <u>had been living</u> in New York for five years when she met Joe.

>The streets were slippery because it <u>had been raining</u> all morning.

To form the past perfect progressive tense, we use the past form of "have", which is "had", along with "been" and the present participle of the main verb.

We form a question in the past perfect progressive tense by changing the word order and starting the question with "had". For example:

<u>Had</u> it <u>been snowing</u> when you arrived home?

To form a negative in the past perfect progressive tense, we add "not" after "had". For example:

It <u>had not been snowing</u> when we got home.

The future perfect progressive tense

We use the future perfect progressive tense to describe an action that will last over a certain period in the future and will have ended by a certain point. For example:

By the time we get to Grandma's house, we <u>will have been driving</u> for three hours and we will be tired.

Grandma <u>will have been baking</u> cookies all morning when we get there.

A time word that we often use with the future perfect progressive tense is "by". For example: **by** the time, **by** tonight, **by** 8 o'clock.

To form the future perfect progressive tense, we use the modal verb "will" along with "have", "been" and the present participle of the main verb. We can also say that we use "will" along with the present perfect progressive tense.

To form a question in the future perfect progressive tense, we change the word order to start the question with "will". For example:

<u>Will</u> Grandma <u>have been waiting</u> for us for a long time by the time by the time we get to her house?

We form the negative in the future perfect progressive tense by adding "not" after "will". For example:

Grandma <u>will not have been waiting</u> for us for too long by the time we get there, because we will probably arrive on time.

Exercise 41

Fill in the correct form of the words in brackets in each of these sentences:

1. I _____ (look) forward to tonight's recital for weeks now.

2. Jill _____ (play) the violin since she was five years old.

3. Julie _____ (busk) in the subway for six months when she met Jill.

4. Jill and Julie _____ (make) music together for three years tonight.

5. Candice plays guitar and _____ (not practice) much recently but maybe tonight will inspire her too.

Lesson 33: Contractions

Contractions are shortened forms of words. For example, "one o'clock" is a shortened form of saying "one of the clock".

To form a contraction, we use an apostrophe to replace the letters that we have dropped to shorten the word. For example, in the contraction "ma'am", which is the shortened form of "madam", the apostrophe replaces the d.

Contractions of verbs

Verb contractions are shortened forms of verbs. Not all verbs have shortened forms but we often use contractions with the different forms of the following verbs: be, have, had, will, would. We normally use them in informal English.

With verb contractions, we usually shorten a verb that goes with a pronoun or a noun. The following table lists the most common verb contractions. The parts that have been dropped to form each contraction are underlined:

Pronoun or noun	be	have	had	will	would
I	I am → I'm	I have → I've	I had → I'd	I will → I'll	I would → I'd
you	you are → you're	you have → you've	you had → you'd	you will → you'll	you would → you'd
he	he is → he's	he has → he's	he had → he'd	he will → he'll	he would → he'd

119

she	she is → she's	she has → she's	she had → she'd	she will → she'll	she would → she'd
it	it is → it's	it has → it's	it had → it'd	it will → it'll	it would → it'd
we	we are → we're	we have → we've	we had → we'd	we will → we'll	we would → we'd
they	they are → they're	they have → they've	they had → they'd	they will → they'll	they would → they'd
who	who is → who's	who has → who's	who had → who'd	who will → who'll	who would → who'd
that	that is → that's	that has → that's	that had → that'd	that will → that'll	that would → that'd
what	what is → what's	what has → what's	what had → what'd	what will → what'll	what would → what'd
where	where is → where's	where has → where's	where had → where'd	where will → where'll	where would → where'd

when	when is → when's	when has → when's	when had → when'd	when will → when'll	when would → when'd
why	why is → why's	why has → why's	why had → why'd	why will → why'll	why would → why'd
how	how is → how's	how has → how's	how had → how'd	how will → how'll	how would → how'd
the dog (or any other common noun)	the dog is → the dog's	the dog has → the dog's	the dog had → the dog'd	the dog will → the dog'll	the dog would → the dog'd
John (or any other proper noun)	John is → John's	John has → John's	John had → John'd	John will → John'll	John would → John'd

Contractions with negatives

It's also common to form contractions with negatives of verbs. When we do this, we follow these steps:

1. We drop the space between the verb and the word "not" to make one word. For example: I do not → I donot
2. We then drop the o in "not" and replace it with an apostrophe. For example: I don*o*t → I don't

The following table lists common contractions of negative forms:

Negative form	Contraction
is not	isn't
are not	aren't
was not	wasn't
were not	weren't
does not	doesn't
do not	don't
did not	didn't
has not	hasn't
have not	haven't
will not	won't
would not	wouldn't
cannot	can't
could not	couldn't
should not	shouldn't
must not	mustn't
might not	mightn't

For the negative form of the modal verb "shall", we drop more than just the o in "not" but we only use the one apostrophe: sha<u>ll</u> n<u>o</u>t → shan't

With contractions of the different negative forms of the verb "be", there are usually two possibilities. For example, we can say "you aren't" but we can also say "you're not". To choose which one to use, we need to decide what we want to emphasize:

- If we want to emphasize the verb, we contract only the verb and "not". For example:

  You <u>aren't</u> going to the party. You're going to stay home instead.

- If we want to emphasize the pronoun or noun, we contract the pronoun and the main verb but leave "not" intact. For example:

  <u>You're</u> not going to the party but Sandy is.

Exercise 42

Rewrite the following paragraph, using shortened forms of the verbs wherever possible:

To make guacamole, you will need an avocado, the juice of a lime, an onion, a bit of garlic and a tomato or two. You will also need a bit of hot sauce and some salt. The avocado should not be hard; it should be ripe and soft. When you are ready, remove the flesh from the avocado and mash it with a fork. Add the lime juice so that the avocado will not turn black. Chop the onion, garlic and tomato until they are fine. Mix the chopped onions, garlic and tomatoes with the mashed avocado until everything has been blended well. Then add a few drops of hot sauce and a little salt. If you do not have the time to chop up everything, you can just use a blender. This will give you a very smooth guacamole.

Lesson 34: Phrasal verbs

Phrasal verbs are verbs that consist of a main verb and a preposition. (We discuss prepositions in Chapter 8.) The preposition can completely change the meaning of the verb. For example:

> Kyle <u>breaks</u> his girlfriend's computer.
>
> When his girlfriend asks who broke the computer, Kyle <u>breaks down</u> and cries.
>
> Kyle's girlfriend is so angry that she doesn't want to be with him anymore and she <u>breaks up</u> with him.

Exercise 43

Use a dictionary to choose the most appropriate phrasal verb in brackets:

Andy _____ (dropped in; dropped out) of high school when he was sixteen years old. He did not want to stay with his strict parents anymore, so he _____ (ran away; ran up; ran into) from home. He would _____ (hang out; hang on; hang up) with a group of older boys who got him _____ (hooked up; hooked on) drugs. To get money for drugs, Andy started _____ (breaking away; breaking into; breaking out) people's houses and stealing their possessions, which he would then sell. Eventually the police caught him and he _____ (ended in; ended up in) jail. His parents felt very _____ (let down; let up) by him.

In prison, Andy managed to _____ (give in; give up) drugs. He started to _____ (work on; work out) in the prison's gym every day and also began to _____ (read out; read up) on health and fitness. When he _____ (got out; got up; got on) after three years, he started his own gym where he would encourage troubled teens to _____ (take up; take on; take down) sport instead of drugs. Finally his parents could feel proud of him!

Chapter 6: Adjectives

Adjectives are words that we use to give more information about nouns or pronouns. For example, they can tell us about the noun's or pronoun's size, shape, color, age and origin. They can tell us what the noun or pronoun is made of, what it is for and what we think of it.

Many adjectives end with suffixes such as the following:

- –an: urban, Indian, American
- –able: adorable, comfortable, available
- –ible: incorrigible, responsible, invisible
- –al: viral, educational, aerial
- –ar: popular, angular, nuclear
- –ic: athletic, scientific, dogmatic
- –ical: identical, magical, comical
- –ine: masculine, feminine, bovine, canine
- –ile: fertile, agile, hostile
- –ive: talkative, furtive, native
- –ent: intelligent, silent, potent
- –ful: beautiful, harmful, deceitful
- –less: careless, useless, timeless
- –ous: dangerous, enormous, fibrous
- –some: handsome, lonesome, awesome

Lesson 35: Attributive, predicative and nominal adjectives

Adjectives can be attributive, predicative or nominal, depending on how we use them in a sentence.

Attributive adjectives

Attributive adjectives usually appear right before the noun or pronoun that they modify. They make up part of the noun phrase or the pronoun phrase and may follow the article or determiner. For example:

> The <u>fluffy</u> cat is sleeping. (The adjective "fluffy" modifies the noun "cat" and follows after the article "the".)

> That <u>black</u> horse is running. (The adjective "black" modifies the noun "horse" and follows after the determiner "that".)

> <u>Lucky </u>you! (The adjective "lucky" modifies the pronoun "you".)

There are some adjectives that we can only use as attributive adjectives in front of a noun. They include: northern, eastern, southern, western, indoor, outdoor.

Predicative adjectives

Predicative adjectives usually come after the noun or pronoun that they modify and we use a linking verb to link them to the noun or pronoun. For example:

> The cat is <u>fluffy</u>. (The verb "is" links the adjective "fluffy" to the noun "cat".)

The horse is <u>black</u>. (The verb "is" links the adjective "black" to the noun "horse".)

You are <u>lucky</u>. (The verb "are" links the adjective "lucky" to the pronoun "you".)

We can use some adjectives only as predicative adjectives. They include: ill, afraid, alone, glad, pleased, thrilled, content, well, alive, asleep, ready, prepared, sorry, bored, annoyed, sure, unable.

Nominal adjectives

Nominal adjectives act almost as nouns, where we leave out the noun. For example:

He likes the blue car but she prefers the <u>green</u>.

Here the word "blue" is an attributive adjective that modifies the noun "car" while "green" is a nominal adjective. It acts as a noun because we left out the noun "car" after "green".

Exercise 44

Identify the adjectives in these sentences and say whether they are attributive, predicative or nominal adjectives:

1. The brown dog is barking loudly.

2. Jane thinks that Mike is handsome.

3. My old grandmother has lost her teeth.

4. Skydiving is only for the brave.

5. The tiny ant in my room is not as scary as the black scorpion.

Lesson 36: Comparison

We can use adjectives to compare different objects or people. To do this, we use the adjectives in their absolute, comparative or superlative forms.

The absolute form

The absolute form of the adjective is the basic form that we use to describe a person, object or group. For example:

>She is smart.

>Sammy's puppy is cute.

>The Blue Mountains are high.

The comparative form

We use the comparative form to describe a person, object or group in comparison to another. It normally describes two people, objects or groups. For example:

>She is smart but her brother is smarter.

>Sammy's puppy is cute but Joey's puppy is cuter.

>The Blue Mountains are high but the Rocky Mountains are higher.

The basic way to make the comparative form of an adjective is to add –er at the end. For example: smart**er**, high**er**, tall**er**.

We only do this for words of one syllable, though. For some words we make the comparative form in a different way:

- Words of one syllable that end in –e: We simply add an r. For example: cute**r**, tame**r**, blue**r**.

- Words of one syllable that end in a vowel and a consonant: We double the consonant and then add –er. For example: big**ger**, mad**der**, red**der**.

- Words of two syllables that end in –y: We take away the y and add –ier. For example: hungr**ier**, clums**ier**, happ**ier**.

- Words of two syllables that do not end in –y and words of three or more syllables: We keep the absolute form but add the word "more" in front of it. For example: **more** playful, **more** intelligent, **more** expensive. There are some exceptions, for example simple**r**.

The superlative form

The superlative form describes a person, object or group that has more of the particular quality than any other of the people, objects or groups we are comparing it to. For example:

> She is smart, her brother is smarter but her sister is the smartest.
>
> Sammy's puppy is cute, Joey's puppy is cuter but Cody's puppy is the cutest.
>
> The Blue Mountains are high, the Rocky Mountains are higher but the Himalayas are the highest.

To make the superlative form, we usually add –est to the adjective if it is a one-syllable word. For example: smart**est**, high**est**, tall**est**.

Like with the comparative form, we make the superlative form of some words in a different way:

- Words of one syllable that end in –e: We simply add an –st. For example: cute**st**, tame**st**, blue**st**.

- Words of one syllable that end in a vowel and a consonant: We double the consonant and then add –est. For example: big**gest**, mad**dest**, red**dest**.

- Words of two syllables that end in –y: We take away the y and add –iest. For example: hungr**iest**, clums**iest**, happ**iest**.

- Words of two syllables that do not end in –y and words of three or more syllables: We keep the absolute form but add the word "most" in front of it. For example: **most** playful, **most** intelligent, **most** expensive. There are some exceptions, such as simple**st**.

Normally we also add an article or a determiner in front of the superlative form. For example: the happiest day, my greatest achievement, that most beautiful of songs.

Adjectives with irregular comparative and superlative forms

A few adjectives are irregular when it comes to their comparative and superlative forms. These include:

Absolute form	Comparative form	Superlative form
good	better	best
bad	worse	worst

131

much	more	most
many	more	most
little	less	least

Other adjectives can be irregular, depending on their meaning. For example:

Absolute form	Comparative form	Superlative form
far	further	furthest
far	farther	farthest

We normally use 'further' and 'furthest' when we talk about a figurative distance, and 'farther' and 'farthest' when we talk about physical distance. However, we can use these forms interchangeably.

Absolute form	Comparative form	Superlative form
old	elder	eldest
old	older	oldest

We use 'elder' and 'eldest' only for people, while we can use 'older' and 'oldest' for animals and things too. Also, when we use 'elder' and 'eldest', it is usually for relatives. For example: my **elder** brother, my **eldest** sister.

Exercise 45

Fill in the correct form of the adjectives in brackets in these sentences:

1. Danny found a _____ (small) shell on the beach. Jared found a _____ (small) shell but Joe found the _____ (small) one.

2. A kitten is _____ (cuddly). A puppy is even _____ (cuddly) but the _____ (cuddly) animal of them all is a panda.

3. Shane is _____ (fit) because he exercises a lot. Kevin is _____ (fit) but James is the _____ (fit).

4. The black cat is _____ (curious). The ginger cat is _____ (curious) but the gray cat is the _____ (curious).

5. Today was a _____ (bad) day. Yesterday was even _____ (bad) but last Monday was the _____ (bad) day of my life!

Lesson 37: The order of adjectives

We do not always use just one adjective to describe someone or something. Often we use two or even more adjectives.

When we use more than one adjective, we usually place one that gives an opinion before one that gives an actual description. For example:

> Jonah is a <u>nice</u> <u>young</u> man.
>
> There is a <u>lovely</u> <u>little</u> <u>old</u> lady who lives down the street.
>
> Cindy does not want to wear the <u>horrible,</u> <u>scratchy</u> <u>red</u> sweater.

Normally we use adjectives in the following order:

1. General opinion, for example: good, bad, nice, lovely, horrible, nasty, strange, wonderful.

2. Specific opinion, for example: delicious, friendly, unfriendly, intelligent, stupid, comfortable, uncomfortable

3. Size, for example: big, small, fat, thin, tall, short

4. Shape, for example: round, square, long

5. Condition or state, for example: dirty, broken, shiny

6. Age, for example: old, ancient, antique, young, new

7. Color, for example: red, blue, green, black

8. Pattern, for example: striped, dotted, flowery

9. Nationality or origin, for example: English, American, Spanish, Chinese, Cherokee, arctic

10. Material, for example: wooden, iron, silk

11. Purpose, for example: hunting, gardening, shopping

An example of a sentence using all these types of adjectives in this order is:

> During her trip, Joanna spent the night in a nice comfortable little round dry old white spotted African mud sleeping hut.

Exercise 46

Place the adjectives in brackets in the correct order:

1. I inherited a (antique, beautiful, silver) bracelet from my grandmother.

2. Johnny is scared of the (big, black, nasty) spider in the bathroom.

3. Iris wore a (blue, floral, Japanese, silk, stylish) dress to the wedding.

4. Drew likes browsing in (dusty, little, quaint) bookstores.

5. Amanda loves dressing up in her grandfather's (beaten-up, brown, flying, leather, old) jacket.

Lesson 38: Adjective phrases

When a string of adjectives describe one noun or pronoun, we can call them an adjective phrase. An adjective phrase is a phrase that acts as an adjective, modifying a noun or pronoun.

Not all adjective phrases consist of several different adjectives. Some consist of an adverb that acts as intensifier, such as 'very', along with an adjective. For example:

> The <u>very friendly</u> sales assistant smiles at all the customers.

In this sentence, 'very friendly' is an adjective phrase because it acts as an adjective to describe the noun, 'sales assistant'. The word 'very' is an adverb that intensifies the adjective 'friendly'.

However, an adjective phrase does not necessarily have to contain an adjective at all. For example:

> Suzie is <u>from Idaho</u>.

In this sentence, the adjective phrase 'from Idaho' acts as a predicative adjective to describe Suzie. It consists of 'from', which is a preposition, and 'Idaho', which is a noun.

Exercise 47

Identify and underline the adjective phrases in these sentences:

1. The incredibly big black bull won first prize at the State Fair.

2. The horse with the black tail is my favorite.

3. The car was far too expensive.

4. People who live near the beach can surf almost every day.

5. The concert will benefit children battling cancer.

Chapter 7: Adverbs

An adverb is a word that modifies or describes a verb, an adjective or another adverb. It can also modify a phrase or a sentence.

Lesson 39: How to identify adverbs

Many adverbs end in the suffix –ly, such as: quickly, slowly, gladly, loudly, quietly. However, not all words that end in –ly are adverbs. For example, 'curly' is usually an adjective, 'assembly' is a noun and 'apply' is a verb.

Furthermore, not all adverbs end in –ly. Some may even look like adjectives at first glance. For example: hard, fast, straight.

In order to correctly identify adverbs, we need to understand the functions of adverbs. They can modify different parts of a sentence. In each example below, the adverb is underlined and the part of the sentence that it modifies is in bold.

Example	Part of sentence modified
The children **play** peacefully.	Verb: "play"
The music is quite **loud**.	Adjective: "loud"
The old man is walking incredibly **slowly**.	Another adverb: "slowly"
It is rather **a lot of food** for one person.	Noun phrase: "a lot of food"
Sarah is going to bed early so she will be ready for tomorrow's race.	Whole clause: "Sarah is going to bed"
Respectfully, that is incorrect.	Whole sentence: "that is incorrect"

Because adverbs can have so many different functions, an easy way to identify them is to remember that they usually answer one of these questions:

- When? For example: Lea <u>always</u> eats breakfast.

- How? For example: Mike eats <u>slowly</u>.

- Where? For example: The dogs eat <u>outside</u>.

- To what extent? For example: Did everyone eat <u>enough</u>?

Exercise 48

Identify and underline the adverbs in these sentences:

1. The dog jumped excitedly into the lake.

2. Alaska is breathtakingly beautiful.

3. John must come home soon because his family misses him.

4. There was trash everywhere after the festival.

5. That was a very nice thing to do for the elderly lady.

Lesson 40: Kinds of adverbs

There are different kinds of adverbs. They are adverbs of time, adverbs of manner, adverbs of place and adverbs of degree.

Adverbs of time

Adverbs of time answer the question "When?" They can tell us when an action happens, how often it happens or for how long it happens.

Examples of adverbs of time are: today, tomorrow, yesterday, later, soon, often, never, always, regularly, monthly, usually, early, late, first, last.

Adverbs of manner

Adverbs of manner answer the question "How?" They tell us about the way in which an action happens.

Examples of adverbs of manner include: quickly, slowly, fast, beautifully, excitedly, neatly, disorderly, sleepily, energetically.

Adverbs of place

Adverbs of place answer the question "Where?" They tell us about the location, direction or distance of an action.

Examples of adverbs of place are: here, there, in, out, inside, outside, everywhere, nowhere, somewhere, upstairs, downstairs, up, down, left, right, north, south, eastwards, westwards, forward, backward, behind, below, above, between, nearby, far.

Adverbs of degree

Adverbs of degree answer the question "To what extent?" They tell us about the degree or the intensity of an action.

Examples of adverbs of degree are: quite, rather, very, too, almost, enough, entirely, hardly, somewhat, extremely, virtually, so, completely, absolutely.

Adverbs of degree can also indicate the comparative or superlative form of an adverb.

- To indicate the comparative form, where we compare two people, animals or things, we add "more" or "less" in front of the adverb. For example: The puppy runs <u>more</u> energetically than the old dog. The old dog runs <u>less</u> energetically than the puppy.

- To indicate the superlative form, where we compare more than two people, animals or things, we add "most" or "least" in front of the adverb. For example: Eddie sings more beautifully than Hilda but Kathy sings the <u>most</u> beautifully. Eddie sings less beautifully than Kathy but Hilda sings the least beautifully.

Some adverbs are irregular in their comparative and superlative forms. For example:

Absolute form	**Comparative form**	**Superlative form**
fast	faster	fastest
well	better	best

Like with adjectives, we usually add an article or determiner in front of the superlative form of an adverb.

Interrogative adverbs

We use the interrogative adverbs to ask questions. Unlike interrogative pronouns, which relate to nouns, interrogative adverbs relate to verbs, adjectives, other adverbs and clauses. The interrogative adverbs are: when, why, where, how.

- When: We use "when" as an interrogative adverb of time. For example:

  <u>When</u> is the train coming?

- Why: We use "why" as an interrogative adverb of reason. For example:

  <u>Why</u> is the train late again?

- Where: We use "where" as an interrogative adverb of place. For example:

  <u>Where</u> is the train?

- How: We can use "how" as an interrogative adverb of time, an interrogative adverb of manner or as an interrogative adverb of degree or quantity. For example:

  <u>How</u> long before the train comes?

  <u>How</u> fast is the train going?

  <u>How</u> late is the train?

  <u>How</u> many more minutes do we have to wait?

Exercise 49

Say what kind of adverb each of the underlined adverbs in these sentences is:

1. The cat is watching the bird <u>intently</u>.

2. <u>How</u> many cookies did she eat?

3. Peter <u>usually</u> goes to bed late at night.

4. I think I left that book <u>somewhere</u> in the living room.

5. I am <u>so</u> tired today.

Exercise 50

Fill in the correct form of the words in brackets:

1. Cindy cooks (well) _____ but Gina cooks (well) _____.

2. John learns (quick) _____. Mike learns in less time than John so he learns (quick) _____ but Jonah, who learns in the least time, learns (quick) _____.

3. A horse runs (fast) _____ than a cow but of all the animals, a cheetah runs (fast) _____.

4. The baby sleeps (peaceful) _____ but its mother tosses and turns all night. She sleeps (peaceful) _____.

5. Jeffrey crosses the street (careful) _____. James crosses the street (careful) _____ because he does not pay as much attention to the traffic as Jeffrey does. Eric does not pay attention to the traffic at all and he crosses the street (careful) _____.

Lesson 41: Forming adverbs from adjectives

We can often form adverbs from adjectives. To do this, we normally add –ly to the end of the adjective. For example:

Adjective	Adverb
beautiful	beautiful**ly**
peaceful	peaceful**ly**
quick	quick**ly**
musical	musical**ly**
loud	loud**ly**

However, we form some adverbs in a different way, depending on how the adjective ends.

- Adjectives that end in –y: When the adjective ends in –y, we form the adverb by changing the y to an i and then adding –ly. For example:

Adjective	Adverb
happy	happ**ily**
cozy	coz**ily**
greedy	greed**ily**

- Adjectives that end in –able or –ible: When the adjective ends in –able or in –ible, we form the adverb by changing the e to a y. For example:

Adjective	Adverb
capable	capably
dependable	dependably
horrible	horribly
terrible	terribly

- Adjectives that end in –ic: When the adjective ends in –ic we form the adverb by adding –ally. For example:

Adjective	Adverb
specific	specifically
basic	basically

Exercise 51

Form adverbs from each of these adjectives:

1. critical
2. regrettable
3. hungry
4. awful
5. thirsty
6. incorrigible
7. truthful
8. economic
9. soft
10. barbaric

Lesson 42: Adverb phrases and adverb clauses

Not all adverbs consist of one word. Adverb phrases and adverb clauses are groups of words that function as an adverb.

Adverb phrases

We can use adverb phrases to tell us more about how, when, where and why or to what extent an action happens. For example:

> Gail acts <u>like a queen</u>.
>
> Shane goes hiking every Saturday morning.
>
> Margie lives in the south of France.
>
> Joseph is studying <u>to become a doctor</u>.
>
> Lee is doing <u>her best</u>.

Adverb clauses

Even though adverb clauses are also groups of words that act as adverbs, they are a little different from adverb phrases:

- Adverb clauses start with a subordinating conjunction, which we discuss in more detail in Chapter 9. These conjunctions are words like "after", "as", "because", "if", "when", "where", "until", "while" and "though". An adverb clause cannot form a sentence on its own but the subordinating conjunction links the clause to the sentence that it depends upon to have meaning.

- Adverb clauses contain a subject and a verb.

Here are some examples of adverb clauses:

If you do not eat enough vegetables, you will not be healthy.

David went on a diet so that he could fit into his new jeans.

<u>Because he loved her</u>, Michael asked Jane to marry him.

After the rain has stopped, we will go for a walk.

<u>No matter how hard she tries</u>, Tracy cannot do a cartwheel.

Exercise 52

Underline the adverb phrases or adverb clauses in these sentences:

1. The cat is sleeping on my lap.

2. The children sing like angels.

3. The boy ran as if his life depended on it.

4. Cecilia looks younger since she lost all that weight.

5. Let's meet for dinner when you have finished work.

Chapter 8: Prepositions

We use prepositions to describe how other words in a sentence relate to one another. They almost never stand alone but usually go with other nouns or gerunds to form prepositional phrases. Examples of prepositions include: on, before, behind, during, at.

Lesson 43: Types of prepositions

The main types of prepositions are prepositions of time, place and direction or movement. Some prepositions can be of more than one type, depending on the words that go with them.

Prepositions of time

The prepositions of time describe, as their name suggests, time. They include prepositions like: during, after, until, before, throughout.

The most common prepositions of time include the following:

- at: We use the preposition "at" for specific times.
  For example:

  I will meet James <u>at</u> noon.

  The bus leaves <u>at</u> 11:30.

- on: We use the preposition "on" for days and dates.
  For example:

  Jeff will arrive <u>on</u> Wednesday.

  Mike's birthday is <u>on</u> January 22.

- in: We use the preposition "in" for times that are not specific but fall within a bigger time period, such as a day, a month, a season or a year. For example:

  It is hard to get up <u>in</u> the morning.

  Mike's birthday is <u>in</u> January.

  Tracy likes to ski <u>in</u> winter.

  Her parents got married <u>in</u> 1983.

- for: We use the preposition "for" when we show a measurement of time. For example:

  Sylvia jogs <u>for</u> an hour every morning.

  We have been friends <u>for</u> years.

- since: We use the preposition "since" with a specific time in the past. For example:

  We have been friends <u>since</u> 2011.

  I have been waiting <u>since</u> breakfast time.

Prepositions of place

We use prepositions of place to describe where something is. There are many different prepositions of place, including: behind, above, beside, below, under.

The prepositions "at", "on" and "in" can be prepositions of place too. For example:

Dorothy and I met <u>at</u> college.

The book is <u>on</u> the table.

There is a spider <u>in</u> the box.

We also use "at", "on" and "in" for these specific purposes:

- at: We use "at" for specific addresses or locations. For example:

  The British Prime Minister lives <u>at</u> 10 Downing Street.

  You need to turn left <u>at</u> the next traffic light.

- on: We use "on" for locations that are not specific but that are along a specific street or road. For example:

  Their house is <u>on</u> Elm Street.

  The church is <u>on</u> the main road.

- in: We use "in" to describe a location within an area of land, such as a town, a country or a continent. For example:

  Jo lives <u>in</u> Anchorage.

  Anchorage is a city <u>in</u> Alaska, which is a state <u>in</u> the United States.

  The United States is <u>in</u> North America.

Prepositions of movement or direction

As their name tells us, we use prepositions of movement or direction to describe where something is moving. They include: to, from, around, up, down, towards.

Exercise 53

Choose the right preposition from the choices in brackets:

1. Tom has been a lawyer _____ (from, since, in) 2008.

2. The horse ran _____ (in, on, at) the meadow.

3. The President lives _____ (in, on, to) Pennsylvania Avenue.

4. Shirley's plane landed _____ (on, at, from) 7 o'clock.

5. Jane ran _____ (at, in, up) the steps to get to class.

Lesson 44: Prepositional phrases

A prepositional phrase is a group of words that contains a preposition. It does not have a verb or a subject but it usually has a preposition with a noun, a pronoun or a gerund. It can have an adjective between the preposition and the noun, pronoun or gerund too.

We use the prepositional phrase to act as an adjective or as an adverb. When it acts as an adjective, it modifies the noun. For example:

> This present is <u>from Grandma</u>. (Here the prepositional phrase "from Grandma" modifies the noun "present", so it acts as an adjective.)

> Grandma lives <u>in the old folks' home</u>. (Here the prepositional phrase "in the old folks' home" acts as an adverb because it modifies the verb "lives".)

Exercise 54

Underline the prepositional phrases in these sentences:

1. The bank manager sits behind a big desk.
2. The squirrel ran down the tree.
3. There are no trains after midnight.
4. Thomas keeps his wallet in his back pocket.
5. I would like to go to the festival.

Lesson 45: Idiomatic expressions with prepositions

There are many different prepositions but in English, certain words always go with certain prepositions to have a specific meaning. We call these phrases idiomatic expressions. There is no easy way to know which preposition goes with a word in an idiomatic expression; we simply have to learn them or use a dictionary.

The following are examples of common idiomatic expressions with prepositions:

afraid <u>of</u>
agree <u>to</u> a proposal
agree <u>with</u> (a person or idea)
agree <u>on</u> a price
agree <u>in</u> principle
angry <u>at</u> (a person)
angry <u>about</u> (a reason)
apologize <u>for</u> (a reason)
apologize <u>to</u> (a person)
approval <u>of</u>
argue <u>about</u> (something)
argue <u>with</u> (a person)
ask <u>about</u>
ask <u>for</u>
aware <u>of</u>
awareness <u>of</u>
belief <u>in</u>

belong to
bring up
capable of
care about (a reason)
care for (a person)
careless about
compare to (to show similarities)
compare with (to show differences)
concern for
confusion about
desire for
differ from (something that is different)
differ with (a person who has a different idea)
familiar with
find out
fond of
fondness for
give up
grasp of
grow up
happy about (a reason)
happy for (a person)
hatred of
hope for
interest in
jealous of
look for

look forward to
look up
love of
made of
make up
married to
need for
participation in
pay for
prepare for
proud of
reason for
respect for
similar to
sorry for
spend on
study for
success in
sure of
talk about
think about
tired of
trust in
understanding of
work for
worried about
worry about

Exercise 55

Fill in the right prepositions in the blank spaces:

Jim is married _____ Lisa. They are preparing _____ a party but Jim is angry _____ Lisa. He is angry _____ the new shoes she bought for the party. They argue _____ this constantly because it seems as if Lisa has no grasp _____ budgeting. However, she cares _____ her appearance and she does not agree _____ Jim that it does not matter what she wears. She wants him to be proud _____ her but she also has a fondness _____ beautiful shoes.

"There was no need _____ an expensive pair of new shoes," Jim says. "Why do you worry _____ how much I spent on shoes?" asks Lisa. "I worked hard _____ the money I used to pay _____ these. They were expensive, yes, but they are made _____ the best leather. You should rather be happy _____ me because I earn enough to buy what I like. Or are you jealous _____ my success because I earn more than you do?"

"Oh, grow _____, Lisa! Why do you bring _____ how much less I earn? I just do not understand why you had to spend so much money _____ shoes that look similar _____ ten other pairs you have already. I apologize _____ getting angry. Let's make _____. I am tired _____ fighting."

Chapter 9: Conjunctions

Conjunctions are "joining words". They link different words, phrases, clauses or sentences together. Examples of conjunctions are: and, but, because, or, so, neither, nor, not only, just as.

Lesson 46: Types of conjunctions

There are three types of conjunctions: coordinating conjunctions, subordinating conjunctions and correlative conjunctions.

Coordinating conjunctions

We use coordinating conjunctions to join together words, phrases, clauses or sentences that are equally important.

There are seven coordinating conjunctions. An easy way to remember them is by using the acronym FANBOYS:

- **f**or: We use "for" in the same way as "because", to explain a reason or a purpose. For example:

    Karl loves traveling, for he likes experiencing new cultures.

- **a**nd: We use "and" to add words or phrases. For example:

    Karl loves traveling and experiencing new cultures.

- **n**or: We use "nor" to show an alternative negative to a negative that we have already stated. For example:

    Karl does not like to stay in the same place nor do the same things every day.

- **b**ut: We use "but" to show contrast. For example:

  Karl loves traveling, but he does not like going on organized tours.

- **o**r: We use "or" to show a choice. For example:

  Karl would like to travel to India or China next.

- **y**et: We use "yet" in a similar way to "but", to show contrast. For example:

  Karl loves traveling, yet he always comes back to his hometown.

- **s**o: We use "so" to show an effect or consequence. For example:

  Karl has traveled to many countries, so he has many stamps in his passport.

We do not normally begin sentences with coordinating conjunctions because when we do, it may seem as if we are just using broken sentences. However, sometimes it is perfectly fine to start a sentence with a coordinating conjunction. For example:

And now it begins ...

When we use a coordinating conjunction to join together independent clauses, we use a comma with the conjunction. For example:

Independent clause: Karl has decided to go to India.

Independent clause: He still has to book a flight.

Joined together: Karl has decided to go to India, but he still has to book a flight.

We do not need to use a comma when a single word or short phrase follows an independent clause. For example:

Karl is going to India and China too.

Subordinating conjunctions

We use a subordinating conjunction to join introduce a dependent clause and link it to an independent clause. A dependent clause is one that cannot stand on its own, even if it looks like a complete sentence. To have meaning, it has to go with an independent clause.

Sometimes the dependent clause comes after the independent clause. For example:

> Karl is going to India (independent clause) <u>even though</u> he does not really like spicy food (dependent clause).

At other times the dependent clause comes before the independent clause. For example:

> <u>Now that</u> Karl has booked his ticket (dependent clause), he is really looking forward to his trip (independent clause).

There are many subordinating conjunctions, including: because, as long as, although, even though, now that, once, until, when, since, while.

Some words may look like subordinating conjunctions but are relative pronouns instead, such as "who", "that" and "which". To tell a subordinating conjunction from a relative pronoun, we need to look at the subject of the dependent clause.

A subordinating conjunction does not act as the subject of the dependent clause. The dependent clause already has a subject. For example:

> Karl is going to India <u>although</u> India is far away.

In the above example, the word "although" is a subordinating conjunction because it does not act as the subject of the dependent clause "although India is far away". The subject of the dependent clause is "India".

A relative pronoun, in contrast, acts as the subject of the dependent clause. For example:

> Karl is going to India, <u>which</u> is far away.

Here the word "which" acts as the subject of the dependent clause, so it is a relative pronoun.

Correlative conjunctions

Correlative conjunctions come in pairs. We use them to join words or phrases that are equally important. Examples of correlative conjunctions are: either/or, neither/nor, not only/but also, rather/or, whether/or, both/and, if/then, as/as.

We use the two correlative conjunctions that make up a pair in different positions in a sentence. For example:

> Karl will fly to <u>either</u> New Delhi <u>or</u> to Mumbai.
>
> A ticket to New Delhi costs <u>as</u> much <u>as</u> a ticket to Mumbai.
>
> <u>Not only</u> will Karl experience India's many cultures, <u>but also</u> its diverse landscapes.
>
> Karl cannot decide <u>whether</u> he should visit India in summer <u>or</u> in winter.

Exercise 56

Underline the conjunctions in these sentences:

1. Sam loves apples <u>and</u> oranges <u>but</u> he hates bananas.

2. Jenny is eating a mango <u>although</u> she would prefer having grapes.

3. <u>Neither</u> Kathy <u>nor</u> Diane likes pineapple.

4. Tammy went to the market <u>where</u> she could not decide <u>whether</u> to buy peaches <u>or</u> strawberries.

5. We bought papaya, pineapple, strawberries <u>and</u> bananas, <u>for</u> we wanted to make a fruit salad for dessert.

Lesson 47: Conjunctive adverbs

Conjunctive adverbs are a special type of adverb or adverbial phrase. While other adverbs modify a word or phrase, conjunctive adverbs simply connect two independent clauses to form one sentence.

There are many different conjunctive adverbs and they have different functions:

- Addition: We use some conjunctive adverbs to show addition. For example: also, in addition.
- Comparison: Some conjunctive adverbs show comparison. For example: similarly, likewise.
- Contrast: We use some conjunctive adverbs to show contrast. For example: however, although, regardless, in spite of. Some conjunctive adverbs come in pairs, for example: one the one hand/on the other hand.
- Concession: Sometimes we use conjunctive adverbs to show concession. For example: granted, of course.
- Time: Some conjunctive adverbs indicate time. For example: next, then, before, after, since, now, meanwhile.
- Emphasis: We can use some conjunctive adverbs to add emphasis. For example: of course, certainly, indeed.
- Explanation: We use certain conjunctive adverbs to explain or illustrate an idea. For example: namely, thus, for instance, for example.
- Summarizing: Some conjunctive adverbs summarize an idea. For example: in conclusion, all in all, that is, finally, in summary.

We normally use a semicolon after the first independent clause because even with the conjunctive adverb, the two clauses could each stand on its own to form a complete sentence. Often we also add a comma after the conjunctive adverb. For example:

> Jennifer did not want to sell her car; <u>however</u>, she needed the money.
>
> Adrian is going to visit London; <u>in addition</u>, he will go to Paris.
>
> There was a storm brewing; <u>consequently</u>, we went home.

Sometimes a word looks like a conjunctive adverb but instead of joining together two independent clauses, it modifies a verb, adjective, adverb or clause. In this case the word is a regular adverb and we do not have to add a semicolon or a comma. For example:

> James <u>finally</u> arrived two hours later.

Here, the word "finally" is an adverb of time because it modifies the verb "arrived".

Exercise 57

Complete these sentences by choosing the most appropriate conjunctive adverb from the options given in brackets:

1. He is a horrible man; _____, he has many friends because he is rich. (consequently; still; likewise)

2. Shane loves to read; _____, he has hundreds of books. (in fact; however; meanwhile)

3. Patricia did not have enough apples for a pie; _____, she used blueberries instead. (for example; so; of course)

4. Janet was cleaning the floor; _____, Andrew and Joe were relaxing on the porch. (otherwise; certainly; at the same time)

5. He is a great pianist; _____, he has been playing the piano since he was five years old. (granted; thus; all in all)

Chapter 10: Interjections

Interjections are often short words that do not have much value in a grammatical sense. However, they can make a big difference to the meaning we want to convey.

We use interjections to show a sudden emotion or a strong feeling, such as surprise, amazement, joy, disgust or confusion.

Lesson 48: How to use interjections

We do not normally use interjections in formal writing but because they are so useful for showing emotion, we often use them in fiction or in informal writing, such as emails to friends.

There are many different interjections in English and we often use an exclamation mark or a comma after the interjection. The interjection can appear in different places in a sentence:

- At the beginning of the sentence: When we use an interjection at the beginning of a sentence, we need to end the sentence with the appropriate punctuation to express the feeling that we want to convey by using the interjection. For example:

  Wow, did you see that?

  Oh no, he's doing it again!

- Elsewhere the sentence: We can use an interjection elsewhere in a sentence too, for instance in the middle or at the end of the sentence. Again, we need to end the sentence with the appropriate punctuation. For example:

He's very good, <u>huh</u>?

When the interjection does not really express a strong emotion, we can simply end the sentence with a full stop. For example:

That is, <u>I would say</u>, the most impressive thing I have ever seen.

- As a separate sentence: We can use many interjections on their own, so that they form a separate sentence. When we do this, we need to use the appropriate punctuation after the interjection and then start the next sentence with a capital letter. For example:

<u>Oh!</u> I never saw that one coming.

<u>What?</u> Did you really have no idea?

<u>So ...</u> Here we go again.

Exercise 58

Underline the interjections in this piece:

Lynsey and Caroline are friends. They are both fifteen years old and, <u>boy</u>, do they have a lot to learn.

Today they are hanging out at the mall and, <u>oh</u>, just watching the shoppers pass by.

"<u>Wow!</u> What is that girl wearing?" Lynsey says.

Caroline replies: "<u>Haha!</u> She looks like, <u>I don't know</u>, my grandmother."

"Those jeans are so, <u>like</u>, last year! <u>Eew!</u>" Lynsey laughs in disgust.

"And that top! <u>Yikes!</u>" Then Caroline hesitates for a moment. "<u>Hey</u>, isn't she Tom's sister? <u>You know</u>, that senior who is just so gorgeous?"

"<u>Hmm</u>, I think you are right. Maybe if we are nice to her, she can introduce us to Tom. <u>Ssh</u>, here she comes. Be nice. <u>Shoot</u>, what is her name again?"

"<u>Uhm</u>, I think it might be Jenny. <u>Darn!</u> I am not sure!"

When the girl reaches them, Lynsey and Caroline put on their biggest smiles. "Hi, how are you ... <u>er</u> ... Jenny? You look, <u>oh</u>, stunning today."

The girl smiles shyly and replies, "<u>Gee</u>, thanks! That is such a nice thing to say. Maybe my brother Tom was wrong about you when he said you were, <u>well</u>, nasty and superficial."

Chapter 11: Check your knowledge

The exercises in this chapter are for you to check your knowledge of English grammar. Check your answers against those given in the "Answers to exercises" section. Each answer has a reference to the relevant lesson, so if you got it wrong, you can go back to that lesson and see why you have made that particular mistake.

Exercise 59

Say what part of speech each of the underlined words in the following story is. You only need to say whether it is a noun, a pronoun, a determiner, a verb, an adjective, an adverb, a preposition, a conjunction or an interjection.

The Iroquois people of (1) <u>North America</u> have a story about how Bear lost his tail. (2) <u>They</u> say that many years ago, Bear had a beautiful long, (3) <u>bushy</u> tail. He was (4) <u>very</u> proud of (5) <u>this</u> tail and loved to show it (6) <u>off</u> to the other animals.

The other animals grew tired of Bear's (7) <u>bragging</u> and one cold winter's day, Fox decided (8) <u>to play</u> a trick on Bear.

Fox knew that Bear loved fish, (9) <u>so</u> he went down to the lake, cut a hole in the ice (10) <u>that</u> covered the lake and put a pile of fish next to the hole. Then he waited for Bear to come to the lake.

(11) <u>When</u> Bear got to the lake, he saw the fish and asked Fox, "Fox, (12) <u>how</u> did you catch so many fish?"

Fox replied, "It's very easy. I (13) <u>will teach</u> you how to do it too, but you must promise to do exactly what I tell (14) <u>you</u>."

Bear (15) eagerly agreed and Fox then took him to another spot, where he cut a new hole in the ice.

"Now, Bear," Fox said. "Just put your tail through this hole and into the water. The fish will see your beautiful tail and will bite onto it with (16) its mouth. But fish can read thoughts, so you must sit very still and think of (17) nothing. I will hide in the bushes over there. When I tell you to, you (18) should pull your tail out and you will have caught a fish."

"(19) That sounds easy," Bear said. So he put his tail into the water, sat very still and thought of nothing. Soon he was (20) fast asleep.

Fox laughed and laughed. When night fell, he went home.

The next morning, Fox came back to the lake. Bear was still sleeping, with (21) snow covering his big body.

Fox (22) quietly crept up to Bear and suddenly shouted into Bear's ear, "Now, Bear! Pull up your tail!"

Bear awoke with a start and tried to pull his tail out of the water. He pulled and pulled but nothing happened. Suddenly there was a loud snap! Bear's tail had broken off because it had frozen (23) into the ice.

"(24) Ouch! Oh! Fox, I will get you for this!" Bear shouted angrily. He jumped at Fox but Fox was (25) much faster and ran away, laughing all the time.

To this day, Bear has a short little stump for a tail and he still doesn't like Fox at all. Do you know why you can sometimes hear Bear groaning in the woods? He groans because he is still sad about losing his beautiful tail.

Exercise 60

Choose the correct word or phrase from each of the options in brackets:

Many cultures (1) _____ (has; have; do have) fables to explain why certain animals look the way they do. In West Africa and the Caribbean, Anansi the spider is a popular character and one story explains how, because of Anansi, spiders have long, thin legs.

Anansi loved good food. One day, he (2) _____ (walk; walked; have walked) past his friend (3) _____ (Rabbit's; Rabbits; Rabbit) house. "Ooh, Rabbit, you are cooking greens!" he cried (4) _____ (excited; more excited; excitedly).

Rabbit replied, "Yes, I (5) _____ (am; are; were). They (6) _____ (have been; are; will be) ready soon. If you wait a little, you can stay and eat with me."

But Anansi knew that if he stayed at Rabbit's house, Rabbit (7) _____ (gives; has given; would give) him a job to do. So he said, "I would love to stay but I can't. I have some errands to run. However, here's what I will do: I will spin (8) _____ (an; a; the) thread and tie one end (9) _____ (on; in; around) my leg. I will then tie the other end of the thread to your pot. (10) _____ (Where; Why; When) the greens are ready, you can tug on the thread and I (11) _____ (came; have come; will come) and eat with you."

Rabbit thought that this was a good plan, (12) _____ (so; nor; but) Anansi spun a thread and tied one end to his leg and the other end to Rabbit's pot.

Anansi continued walking. Soon he smelled some beans cooking. The (13) _____ (monkeys; monkey's) were making beans for their dinner.

"Hello, Anansi! Come and eat with (14) _____ (we; our; us). Our beans are almost ready."

Again, Anansi said that he would spin a thread so that the monkeys could let him know when the beans were ready. The monkeys thought this was (15) _____ (an; a; the) excellent plan, so once again Anansi spun a thread, then tied one end to one of his legs and the other end to the (16) _____ (monkeys; monkey's; monkeys') pot.

Anansi walked a little further and now he smelled sweet potatoes cooking. As he sniffed the (17) _____ (delicious; deliciously) aroma, his friend Hog called out to him, "Anansi, I know how much you like sweet potatoes and honey. The dish is almost ready. (18) _____ (You stay; Will you stay; Have you stayed) and eat with me?"

Anansi said, "That would be very nice, Hog, but I (19) _____ (may run; can run; have to run) a few errands first." Once again he spun a thread and tied one end to one of his legs, with the other end tied to Hog's pot.

As Anansi was walking down to the river, he met more neighbors along the way and everybody invited him for a meal. By the time the spider got to the river, he had a thread tied to each of his eight legs.

"Oh, I am so clever," he thought. "I wonder what I (20) _____ (eat; ate; will be eating) first."

Suddenly Anansi felt a tug at one of his legs. "Ah, that is the thread tied to Rabbit's pot. I will be having greens first then."

The next moment there was a tug at one of Anansi's other legs. And then came a tug at a third leg, and then at a fourth, and a fifth, a sixth, then a seventh. "Oh no," Anansi thought as he felt a tug at his eighth leg.

He was being pulled in all directions at once. He (21) _____ (should feel; may feel; could feel) his long legs stretching and stretching, becoming (22) _____ (long; longer; longest) and thinner as his neighbors (23) _____ (pull; would pull; were pulling) on the threads all at the same time.

"What will I do?" he cried.

Anansi then jumped in the river. The water washed away all the threads and Anansi was free again. He dragged (24) _____ (his; him; himself) out of the water and onto the river bank, where he then (25) _____ (lie; lied; lay) panting.

"Oops! That was not such a great idea after all."

To this day, Anansi's spider children and grandchildren have long, thin legs.

Answers to exercises

Exercise 1

Common nouns	Proper nouns
door	Madagascar
lion	Cookie Monster
rain	Pizza Hut
guitar hero	Guitar Hero
basil	Basil

Exercise 2

1. friend: common noun
   Jill: proper noun
   basketball: common noun

2. Amritsar: proper noun
   Golden Temple: proper noun

3. Michael: proper noun
   Game of Thrones: proper noun
   television: common noun
   Sunday: proper noun

4. aunt: common noun
   Day of Atonement: proper noun

5. Love: common noun
   feeling: common noun

Exercise 3

1. dog: concrete noun

2. craving: abstract noun

    chocolate: concrete noun

3. childhood: abstract noun

    joy: abstract noun

    love: abstract noun

4. truth: abstract noun

5. mother: concrete noun

    justice: abstract noun

    democracy: abstract noun

    freedom: abstract noun

    dignity: abstract noun

Exercise 4

1. fly: countable noun

    ceiling: countable noun

2. boy: countable noun

    glass: countable noun

    milk: uncountable noun

3. friend: countable noun

    box: countable noun

    cookies: uncountable noun

4. sand: uncountable noun

    beach: countable noun

5. sandwich: countable noun

    butter: uncountable noun

    slice: countable noun

    cheese: uncountable noun

Exercise 5

1. dogs
2. chairs
3. trays
4. umbrellas
5. beehives
6. mongooses
7. halves
8. fungi
9. firemen
10. nannies
11. jellies
12. oases
13. appendices
14. memoranda
15. lives
16. wolves
17. puppies
18. boxes
19. daisies
20. aircraft

Exercise 6

1. A pack of dogs
2. A fleet of airplanes
3. A bale of turtles
4. A range of mountains
5. A crew of sailors

Exercise 7

1. feminine
2. common
3. neuter
4. common
5. masculine
6. masculine
7. feminine
8. common
9. neuter
10. common

Exercise 8

1. count
2. heroine
3. angeline
4. jill
5. hen
6. czarina
7. mare
8. billy
9. ewe
10. monk

Exercise 9

1. window shopping
2. Valentine's Day
3. road trip; Blue Mountains
4. blackbird
5. winter sports; snow-boarding; cross-country skiing

Exercise 10

1. storeroom
2. dress size
3. window frame
4. pet food
5. heart surgeon

Exercise 11

1. bridegrooms
2. birthday presents
3. bucketfuls
4. assistant football coaches
5. ladies-in-waiting

Exercise 12

1. Mandy
2. Mandy; Joe
3. Mandy; friend
4. Mandy; friend
5. Joe; man

Exercise 13

1. *Game of Thrones*
2. popcorn
3. popcorn
4. Stuart; popcorn; *Game of Thrones*; television
5. pizza

Exercise 14

1. Tom's
2. Rachel's
3. restaurant's
4. servers'; Tom's
5. Rachel's

Exercise 15

1. Barbara's
2. dog's; cat's
3. dog and cat's
4. dog's and cat's
5. neighbors'; Spot and Socks's or Spot and Socks'

Exercise 16

1. She; it
2. We; They
3. you; It
4. They; us; We; them
5. you, it

Exercise 17

1. his
2. yours
3. ours
4. theirs
5. hers

Exercise 18

1. I cannot believe <u>this</u>!
2. Are <u>these</u> your keys?
3. <u>That</u> was so much fun!
4. <u>Those</u> are the shoes that I want.
5. These apples look a little rotten. <u>Those</u> look much fresher.

Exercise 19

1. <u>Somebody</u> is playing loud music.
2. How would <u>one</u> bake a cake without an oven?
3. Come on, <u>everybody</u>, let's do <u>something</u> about this!
4. I don't want to eat <u>anything</u>. <u>Neither</u> does she.
5. Both boys are twelve years old. <u>Both</u> love riding their bicycles.

Exercise 20

I was really excited about going to the party. <u>Who</u> would be there? <u>Whom</u> would I meet?

The entire afternoon I spent wondering <u>what</u> to wear. <u>Which</u> dress would be more flattering: the green one or the red one? <u>Which</u> shoes would be the most comfortable for dancing in but would still look great? How would I do my hair? Would I wear it in a ponytail, a bun or just let it flow loosely over my shoulders?

When I finally got dressed and was ready to go, disaster struck! Where were my keys? They were not where I always left them on the table by the front door. <u>Whosoever</u> could have taken them? I searched and searched, knowing that if I didn't find my keys soon, I would not be able to go at all. <u>What</u> would my friends think? How would the birthday girl feel if I didn't show up?

After what felt like hours, I heard something tinkling in the living room. <u>Whatever</u> could that be? I went to take a look and there, playing with my bunch of keys, was the biggest ginger cat I had ever seen. Now I had something new to worry about: <u>Whose</u> cat was it?

Exercise 21

1. who
2. that
3. whose
4. which
5. whom

Exercise 22

1. which/that
2. which/that
3. whose
4. which/that
5. whose

Exercise 23

1. himself
2. myself
3. themselves
4. ourselves
5. yourself

Exercise 24

1. intensive
2. reflexive
3. reflexive
4. intensive
5. reflexive; intensive

Exercise 25

1. one another
2. each other's
3. each other; each other
4. each other
5. one another's

Exercise 26

1. a; the; The; a
2. an; a
3. the; a
4. the; an
5. a; an; the

Exercise 27

<u>These</u> days, I prefer to spend Friday night at home with a good book or a movie. Sometimes I will treat myself and order one of <u>those</u> pizzas with every topping I can think of and some extra cheese. This is my idea of a party now that I'm older.

Back when I was a student in my twenties, <u>this</u> kind of Friday night was my biggest nightmare. Weekends were party time! I will always remember <u>that</u> time when we went to a music festival and danced to <u>this</u> band that played the craziest music with fiddles and didgeridoos. It was freezing <u>that</u> night but we stayed warm simply by dancing until sunrise. Those were the days!

Exercise 28

1. some
2. much
3. each
4. neither
5. All; few of the

Exercise 29

1. his
2. her
3. Its
4. your
5. Their

Exercise 30

1. love: stative
2. are fishing: action
3. drinks: stative; is drinking: action
4. are feeling: action
5. weighs: action; weigh: stative

Exercise 31

1. hits: transitive
2. cheer: intransitive
3. buys: transitive
4. tastes: intransitive
5. does not like: transitive
6. prefers: intransitive
7. prefers: transitive
8. is watching: transitive
9. is watching: intransitive
10. love: intransitive

Exercise 32

1. began; begun
2. ate; ate
3. loved; loved
4. relied; relied
5. repelled; repelled
6. repealed; repealed
7. threw; thrown
8. set; set
9. boggled; boggled
10. ran; run

Exercise 33

Doron asked Rachel <u>to marry</u> him last month. They plan <u>to have</u> their wedding in July. Rachel would like a small wedding with only a few guests but Doron wants all their friends and family <u>to come</u>. This is not the only thing that they disagree on. For instance, Rachel would love <u>to have</u> a chocolate wedding cake while Doron would prefer <u>to have</u> a vanilla cake instead. Luckily they have learned that <u>to compromise</u> is one of the most important ingredients for a successful marriage. They will have <u>to work</u> through their differences and find a solution that will work for both of them. At least they are both looking forward to being partners for the rest of their lives.

Exercise 34

1. go; goes
2. Does
3. am; is; are
4. has; had
5. was; were

Exercise 35

1. howling
2. spying
3. shopping
4. coping
5. belying
6. occurring
7. pampering
8. dying
9. dyeing
10. arguing

Exercise 36

Uncle Jim and Aunt Sally have three children. Peter, the eldest, <u>is</u> working with Doctors Without Borders in the Middle East. Paul is the middle child and he <u>is</u> studying. He <u>does</u> not want to become a doctor like his brother but instead he <u>is</u> studying to become a teacher. What <u>does</u> the youngest, Mary, do? She <u>has</u> finished high school and <u>has</u> joined the military.

Exercise 37

As a little girl, Diana <u>would</u> dream of becoming a ballerina. Now that she is all grown up, she knows that she <u>ought to</u> focus on other dreams instead. She is too clumsy to be a graceful dancer but she <u>can</u> sing beautifully. She <u>should</u> enter that talent competition on television. After all, she <u>could</u> do very well.

Exercise 38

1. am
2. bit
3. bit; was; did not hurt
4. will take
5. Will you remember

Exercise 39

1. are planning
2. Will they be visiting
3. was eating
4. was not carrying; was raining
5. will be shining

Exercise 40

1. has opened
2. had had
3. Have you ever eaten
4. has never liked
5. will have remembered

Exercise 41

1. have been looking
2. has been playing
3. had been busking
4. will have been making
5. has not been practicing

Exercise 42

To make guacamole, <u>you'll</u> need an avocado, the juice of a lime, an onion, a bit of garlic and a tomato or two. <u>You'll</u> also need a bit of hot sauce and some salt. The avocado <u>shouldn't</u> be hard; it should be ripe and soft. When <u>you're</u> ready, remove the flesh from the avocado and mash it with a fork. Add the lime juice so that the avocado <u>won't</u> turn black. Chop the onion, garlic and tomato until <u>they're</u> fine. Mix the chopped onions, garlic and tomatoes with the mashed avocado until <u>everything's</u> been blended well. Then add a few drops of hot sauce and a little salt. If you <u>don't</u> have the time to chop up everything, you can just use a blender. <u>This'll</u> give you a very smooth guacamole.

Exercise 43

Andy <u>dropped out</u> of high school when he was sixteen years old. He did not want to stay with his strict parents anymore, so he <u>ran away</u> from home. He would <u>hang out</u> with a group of older boys who got him <u>hooked on</u> drugs. To get money for drugs, Andy started <u>breaking into</u> people's houses and stealing their possessions, which he would then sell. Eventually the police caught him and he <u>ended up in</u> jail. His parents felt very <u>let down</u> by him.

In prison, Andy managed to <u>give up</u> drugs. He started to <u>work out</u> in the prison's gym every day and also began to <u>read up</u> on health and fitness. When he <u>got out</u> after three years, he started his own gym where he would encourage troubled teens to <u>take up</u> sport instead of drugs. Finally his parents could feel proud of him!

Exercise 44

1. brown: attributive
2. handsome: predicative
3. old: attributive
4. brave: nominal
5. tiny: attributive; scary: predicative; black: attributive

Exercise 45

1. small; smaller; smallest
2. cuddly; cuddlier; cuddliest
3. fit; fitter; fittest
4. curious; more curious; most curious
5. bad; worse; worst

Exercise 46

1. beautiful, antique, silver
2. nasty, big, black
3. stylish, blue, floral, Japanese, silk
4. quaint, little, dusty
5. beaten-up, old, brown, leather, flying

Exercise 47

1. The <u>incredibly big black</u> bull won first prize at the State Fair.
2. The horse <u>with the black tail</u> is my favorite.
3. The car was far too expensive.
4. People <u>who live near the beach</u> can surf almost every day.
5. The concert will benefit children <u>battling cancer</u>.

Exercise 48

1. The dog jumped <u>excitedly</u> into the lake.
2. Alaska is <u>breathtakingly</u> beautiful.
3. John must come home <u>soon</u> because his family misses him.
4. There was trash <u>everywhere</u> after the festival.
5. That was a <u>very</u> nice thing to do for the elderly lady.

Exercise 49

1. Adverb of manner
2. Interrogative adverb
3. Adverb of time
4. Adverb of place
5. Adverb of degree

Exercise 50

1. well; better
2. quickly; more quickly; the most quickly
3. faster; the fastest
4. peacefully; less peacefully
5. carefully; less carefully; the least carefully

Exercise 51

1. critically
2. regrettably
3. hungrily
4. awfully
5. thirstily
6. incorrigibly
7. truthfully
8. economically
9. softly
10. barbarically

Exercise 52

1. The cat is sleeping <u>on my lap</u>.
2. The children sing <u>like angels</u>.
3. The boy ran as if his life depended on it.
4. Cecilia looks younger since she lost all that weight.
5. Let's meet for dinner when you have finished work.

Exercise 53

1. since
2. in
3. on
4. at
5. up

Exercise 54

1. The bank manager sits <u>behind a big desk</u>.
2. The squirrel ran <u>down the tree</u>.
3. There are no trains <u>after midnight</u>.
4. Thomas keeps his wallet <u>in his back pocket</u>.
5. I would like to go <u>to the festival</u>.

Exercise 55

Jim is married <u>to</u> Lisa. They are preparing <u>for</u> a party but Jim is angry <u>at</u> Lisa. He is angry <u>about</u> the new shoes she bought for the party. They argue <u>about</u> this constantly because it seems as if Lisa has no grasp <u>of</u> budgeting. However, she cares <u>about</u> her appearance and she does not agree <u>with</u> Jim that it does not matter what she wears. She wants him to be proud <u>of</u> her but she also has a fondness <u>for</u> beautiful shoes.

"There was no need <u>for</u> an expensive pair of new shoes," Jim says. "Why do you worry <u>about</u> how much I spent on shoes?" asks Lisa. "I worked hard <u>for</u> the money I used to pay <u>for</u> these. They were expensive, yes, but they are made <u>of</u> the best leather. You should rather be happy <u>for</u> me because I earn enough to buy what I like. Or are you jealous <u>of</u> my success because I earn more than you do?"

"Oh, grow <u>up</u>, Lisa! Why do you bring <u>up</u> how much less I earn? I just do not understand why you had to spend so much money <u>on</u> shoes that look similar <u>to</u> ten other pairs you have already. I apologize <u>for</u> getting angry. Let's make <u>up</u>. I am tired <u>of</u> fighting."

Exercise 56

1. Sam loves apples <u>and</u> oranges <u>but</u> he hates bananas.
2. Jenny is eating a mango <u>although</u> she would prefer having grapes.
3. <u>Neither</u> Kathy <u>nor</u> Diane likes pineapple.
4. Tammy went to the market where she could not decide <u>whether</u> to buy peaches <u>or</u> strawberries.
5. We bought papaya, pineapple, strawberries <u>and</u> bananas, <u>for</u> we wanted to make a fruit salad for dessert.

Exercise 57

1. still
2. in fact
3. so
4. at the same time
5. granted

Exercise 58

Lynsey and Caroline are friends. They are both fifteen years old and, <u>boy</u>, do they have a lot to learn.

Today they are hanging out at the mall and, <u>oh</u>, just watching the shoppers pass by.

"<u>Wow</u>! What is that girl wearing?" Lynsey says.

Caroline replies: "<u>Haha</u>! She looks like, <u>I don't know</u>, my grandmother."

"Those jeans are so, <u>like</u>, last year! Eew!" Lynsey laughs in disgust.

"And that top! <u>Yikes</u>!" Then Caroline hesitates for a moment. "<u>Hey</u>, isn't she Tom's sister? <u>You know</u>, that senior who is just so gorgeous?"

"<u>Hmm</u>, I think you are right. Maybe if we are nice to her, she can introduce us to Tom. <u>Ssh</u>, here she comes. Be nice. <u>Shoot</u>, what is her name again?"

"<u>Uhm</u>, I think it might be Jenny. <u>Darn</u>! I am not sure!"

When the girl reaches them, Lynsey and Caroline put on their biggest smiles. "<u>Hi</u>, how are you ... <u>er</u> ... Jenny? You look, <u>oh</u>, stunning today."

The girl smiles shyly and replies, "<u>Gee</u>, thanks! That is such a nice thing to say. Maybe my brother Tom was wrong about you when he said you were, <u>well</u>, nasty and superficial."

Exercise 59

1. Noun (Lesson 1)
2. Pronoun (Lesson 9)
3. Adjective (Lesson 35)
4. Adverb (Lesson 39)
5. Determiner (Lesson 18)
6. Preposition (Lesson 45)
7. Noun (Lesson 26)
8. Verb (Lesson 24)
9. Conjunction (Lesson 46)
10. Pronoun (Lesson 14)
11. Conjunction (Lesson 46)
12. Interrogative adverb (Lesson 40)
13. Verb (Lesson 29)
14. Pronoun (Lesson 9)
15. Adverb (Lesson 39)
16. Pronoun (Lesson 10)
17. Pronoun (Lesson 12)
18. Verb (Lesson 28)
19. Pronoun (Lesson 11)
20. Adverb (Lesson 39)
21. Noun (Lesson 1, Lesson 2 and Lesson 3)
22. Adverb (Lesson 39)
23. Preposition (Lesson 43)
24. Interjection (Lesson 48)
25. Adverb (Lesson 39 and Lesson 40)

Exercise 60

1. have (Lesson 25)
2. walked (Lesson 29)
3. Rabbit's (Lesson 8)
4. excitedly (Lesson 41)
5. am (Lesson 25 and Lesson 30)
6. will be (Lesson 29)
7. would give (Lesson 28)
8. a (Lesson 17)
9. around (Lesson 43)
10. When (Lesson 46)
11. will come (Lesson 29)
12. so (Lesson 46)
13. monkeys (Lesson 4)
14. us (Lesson 9)
15. an (Lesson 17)
16. monkeys' (Lesson 8)
17. delicious (Lesson 35)
18. Will you stay (Lesson 29)
19. have to run (Lesson 28)
20. will be eating (Lesson 30)
21. could feel (Lesson 28)
22. longer (Lesson 36)
23. were pulling (Lesson 30)
24. himself (Lesson 15)
25. lay (Lesson 23 and Lesson 29)

Conclusion

We hope that this book has helped you to gain a better understanding of English grammar. You now know how to use the different parts of speech correctly and sound like a native English speaker.

The next step is to keep practicing English and to refer to this book as well as your dictionary whenever you write something in English. You may want to explore the online grammar resources listed in Chapter 1 for more grammar exercises. Once you feel confident about how to use the different parts of speech, you may also want to learn more about other aspects of English grammar, such as punctuation rules.

Printed in Dunstable, United Kingdom